Don't Gobble the Marshmallow ... Ever!

The Secret to Sweet Success in Times of Change

Joachim de Posada
and Ellen Singer

BERKLEY BOOKS, NEW YORK

THE BERKLEY PUBLISHING GROUP
Published by the Penguin Group
Penguin Group (USA) Inc.
375 Hudson Street, New York, New York 10014, USA
Penguin Group (Canada), 90 Eglinton Avenue East, Suite 700, Toronto, Ontario M4P 2Y3, Canada
(a division of Pearson Penguin Canada Inc.)
Penguin Books Ltd., 80 Strand, London WC2R 0RL, England
Penguin Group Ireland, 25 St. Stephen's Green, Dublin 2, Ireland (a division of Penguin Books Ltd.)
Penguin Group (Australia), 250 Camberwell Road, Camberwell, Victoria 3124, Australia
(a division of Pearson Australia Group Pty. Ltd.)
Penguin Books India Pvt. Ltd., 11 Community Centre, Panchsheel Park, New Delhi—110 017, India
Penguin Group (NZ), 67 Apollo Drive, Rosedale, North Shore 0632, New Zealand
(a division of Pearson New Zealand Ltd.)
Penguin Books (South Africa) (Pty.) Ltd., 24 Sturdee Avenue, Rosebank, Johannesburg 2196,
South Africa

Penguin Books Ltd., Registered Offices: 80 Strand, London WC2R 0RL, England

This book is an original publication of The Berkley Publishing Group.

The publisher does not have any control over and does not assume any responsibility for author or third-party websites or their content.

Copyright © 2007 by Joachim de Posada, Ph.D., and Ellen Singer.
Cover design and art by Sawsan Chalabi.
Interior text design by Tiffany Estreicher.

FIRST EDITION: November 2007

Library of Congress Cataloging-in-Publication Data

Posada, Joachim de.
  Don't gobble the marshmallow . . . ever! : the secret to sweet success in times of change /
Joachim de Posada and Ellen Singer. — 1st ed.
    p. cm.
  ISBN 978-0-425-21742-9
  1. Success. 2. Goal (Psychology) 3. Career development. 4. Success in business. I. Singer,
Ellen, 1957–   II. Title.

BF637.S8P59846 2007
650.1—dc22   2007029160

PRINTED IN THE UNITED STATES OF AMERICA

10 9 8 7 6 5 4 3 2 1

Most Berkley Books are available at special quantity discounts for bulk purchases for sales promotions, premiums, fund-raising, or educational use. Special books, or book excerpts, can also be created to fit specific needs.

For details, write: Special Markets, The Berkley Publishing Group,
375 Hudson Street, New York, New York 10014.

Joachim:

This book is dedicated to my daughter, Caroline, who just graduated from law school and passed the very difficult bar exam. She is now a very successful attorney. I am so proud of her.

And to Victoria, my partner in life who gave me her unconditional love and understanding when I needed it the most.

Ellen:

For B, K & W, my wise, wickedly funny and wonderfully supportive ladies, and D, whose amazing spirit unfailingly keeps my own aloft. And also for my mom, who let me read books *before* cleaning my room, teaching me the importance of setting priorities based on passions rather than practicalities.

Acknowledgments

Joachim:

I would like to express my sincere appreciation to all the brilliant leaders, mentors, coaches, teachers and executives from whom I have learned so much and the millions of people who have attended my speeches, workshops and seminars over the years. I am very grateful because I have learned from all of you.

Special thanks to readers in South Korea, Taiwan, Japan, Thailand, Greece, Turkey, Denmark, China, Spain, Brazil, Central and South America, as well as those in the United States and Puerto Rico, where I live and work. You have made *Don't Eat the Marshmallow . . . Yet!* a worldwide bestseller and given us reason to write this sequel to the original story. I have visited many of your countries to speak and sign books and you have provided me with experiences I will never forget. I hope this book is very useful to you all and, in some small way, influences your life and the lives of your loved ones.

Thanks to Ellen Singer, my coauthor, for collaborating on this book with me. You are an awesome writer, mother and colleague and I am proud to work with you.

Thanks to Denise Silvestro, Katherine Day, Tim Taylor, Lance Fitzgerald, and Berkley president Leslie Gelbman for working with us on the hardest job of all, which is polishing, publicizing and distributing the book so that people can buy it and read it. Thank you for giving us the opportunity to write the first book and now this one.

Thanks to Yahoo! in Latin America, the *San Juan Star* and WOSO for having me as a regular contributor and to CNN,

Univision, Telemundo, TV Azteca, TV America, the *New York Times*, *Hispanic Business*, *Hispanic Trends* and *Hispanic* magazine and all other media who have invited me to talk about my books and professional activities.

Thanks to my professional partners, Ramon Arias, from Interamerican Management Consultants; Rick Fernandez, from the Advent Group; Pierce and Jane Howard, from Centacs; and Alan Mcabeea and Ariel Coro.

Thanks to Professor Clemente Vivanco, who has been by my side in the good and bad times.

Thanks to my family, the Posadas and the Beguiristains, for always being there.

Ellen:

Even the most gracious *thank-you* fails to capture deep appreciation so, with apologies for such inescapable inadequacy, I offer sincerest gratitude to:

My daughters, who tirelessly answered my many and, sometimes, odd research questions—even at three in the morning—and who triple- and quadruple-checked every detail;

Evan Hamilton and Aaron Araki, for sharing their passion and expertise about guitars and music;

Jane, Miriam, and the staff of Dystel & Goderich Literary Management, for giving me support, kindness and a much-treasured travel mug;

Denise Silvestro, Katherine Day and everyone at The Berkley Publishing Group for making the post-writing experience nearly as rewarding as the work itself;

Scott Schwimer, my Dudley Do-Right entertainment lawyer, who is always ready to save my day; and

A cryptic pair—someone who is a bit brash and hugs a lot like Charley—for their very clear and unified friendship.

Contents

Joachim's Pre-Parable Analysis   1

1. Big (Marshmallow) Man on Campus   7

2. Marshmallow Madness   17

3. Stressed—and Stretched—to Impress   34

4. The Fall from Marshmallow Grace   42

5. Wages and Wagers   55

6. Back to Marshmallow Basics   65

7. Dinner with Jonathan Patient   78

8. The One-Minute Success Quiz   91

9. The Laws of Life   111

10. The Secret Inside the Envelope   119

Joachim's Post-Parable Analysis   126

Authors' Note   164

Joachim's Pre-Parable Analysis

Many people who have stopped to ask for directions have been told, at least once, that "you can't get there from here."

Most of us, hearing this discouraging news, turn around and go home. Or maybe we settle for a new destination—a bar or a shopping mall—to kill the time we'd allotted to getting *there*.

But successful people don't worry about getting from their current to their desired locations. They don't focus on getting from *here* to *there*. They concentrate on the *there* part and find ways under, around, over and through any obstacles in their paths.

This book will give you a new way of thinking about and achieving your goals. More important, it will show you how to sustain success throughout your life, how to adjust to negative and positive changes—both the potholes and the super-speed highways—so that your journey and your desired destination remain linked.

It all depends on what you do with your marshmallows.

For instance, what would you choose: a million dollars today or a billion dollars in five years? Sex now with the hottest person in the room or sex a year from now and the rest of your life thereafter with the person of your dreams? A vending machine candy bar right this minute or a pound of the world's finest chocolate next week? Do you live from payday to payday or put away a portion of every dollar you earn so that you can enjoy a comfortable retirement?

Do you seek immediate satisfaction or hold out for what will give you greater long-term happiness? Are you like the average American who saves less than one percent of his disposable income each year? Do you eat your marshmallows every chance you get, gobbling them during times of change, or save and savor them throughout your life?

Don't Gobble the Marshmallow . . . Ever! is a lighthearted parable wrapped around a rock-solid principle:

the ability to delay gratification leads to sustained success in work and life. The fictional tale is based on real-life experiences of the authors and a forty-year-old Stanford University study. Children were left alone in a room each with a marshmallow and given the choice of eating it then or fifteen minutes later, when they were promised an extra marshmallow as a reward for waiting. Some ate theirs right away. Others waited. But the study's real significance came fourteen years later when the researchers discovered that the children who held out for the reward had become more successful than the children who had eaten their marshmallows immediately.*

This story begins with Arthur, whom you may have met in my previous book, *Don't Eat the Marshmallow . . . Yet!*, graduating from college. Although the former chauffeur has been learning, practicing and preaching the marshmallow principle for five years, his goal-seeking practices fall apart when his life becomes irrevocably altered by . . . success! That's right—getting what we want (or think we want) can be as uncomfortable, distracting and depressing as failure.

Whether you are experiencing an obvious life change—

---

*To watch a segment of the marshmallow experiment conducted by Joachim with four-, five-, and six-year-olds, go to www.marshmallow book.com.

graduation, marriage or divorce—or a more subtle change in values, perspective or health, the marshmallow theory is something you can learn (or relearn with Arthur, his college friends, a waitress who aspires to restaurant ownership, a teen who wants to be a rock star and a mother so focused on her children that she has no goals of her own) and apply to your own personal definition of success.

The situations in the parable are also based on real-life experiences. Just like Arthur, I celebrated my first taste of success by spending more than I could afford (on homes, decorators, cars and women). I never had trouble making money; my problem was holding on to my earnings. The higher the income, the greater my debt. Determined to change my fate, I made it my mission to discover the key ingredient to sustained, lifelong success. When I found that the ability to delay gratification was the *one* habit shared by every person I studied, I began applying the marshmallow principle to my own life.

Today, I enjoy the luxury only one in four Americans expects to attain—financial security. I could retire today and live comfortably for the rest of my life. Retirement is the last thing on my mind—I am passionate about spreading the marshmallow word and will continue to share its secrets of success as a motivational speaker and writer until the day I die—but it is extremely rewarding to know that working is a choice rather than a necessity.

It is never too late to receive the rewards of delayed gratification—I was in my late thirties when I started practicing the marshmallow principle—and it is never impossible to return to your goals no matter how far you've veered off the path to success.

The experiences of Ellen Singer, for instance, illustrate this book's subtitle, *The Secret to Sweet Success in Times of Change.* Unlike me, my coauthor was a marshmallow-resisting natural as a young adult. She put herself through college and, by the time she earned her master's degree at age twenty-three, she had also saved enough money to buy a new car and afford a down payment on a house. A self-proclaimed master of the five-year plan, she set—and achieved—goals including on-target promotions and carefully planned pregnancies.

But when Ellen's circumstances changed and she ended an abusive marriage, she didn't adjust her goals—she abandoned them. As she puts it, "I couldn't even master a five-day plan. It was more like five minutes. If someone asked me what I was doing for the weekend, I'd say, 'Ask me on Saturday.' For nearly a decade my savings consisted of spare change and soda-bottle deposit money, and my goal of becoming an author seemed like a sad joke."

How did I secure financial independence after years of eating my marshmallows and how did Ellen get back on her marshmallow-resisting track? We'll share the details in the Post-Parable Analysis, where we will also give you step-by-step guidance to The Six-Step Marshmallow Plan to Sweet Success in Anything—and Everything! and The Ten-Step Master Marshmallow Plan for Sustained Success in Times of Change. (For more information, visit www.marshmallow.com.)

Don't Gobble the Marshmallow . . .Ever! will also reveal a very important secret of success revealed to me by a billion-dollar author. I hope the secret, introduced in the parable as a graduation present from Jonathan Patient to Arthur, and the marshmallow principle open your eyes wide, engross your imagination and encourage you to think big, aim high and go for whatever you want in life.

I hope you are entertained, enlightened and inspired by the stories told in the parable. Arthur's new predicament should make you laugh, but the fluffy marshmallow principle is serious, lifelong stuff. This book will help you delay gratification to reach your career and life goals and enjoy the sweet rewards of your success without gobbling your marshmallow dreams.

1

Big (Marshmallow) Man on Campus

"Now, remember, marshmallows don't grow on trees," Arthur playfully admonished his cap-and-gowned audience. "But for this year's marshmallow-resisting graduates of the University of Miami, they *do* fall from the sky!"

On cue, nearly a million orange, green and white miniature marshmallows dropped from a crop duster flying over the Barek United Center and between the blinding barrage of school-colored candy and celebratory cheering of students dressed in clothes of similar hues, no one noticed Arthur's briefly furrowed brow as he moved from behind the lectern to exit the stage.

Almost no one. Jonathan Patient, a billionaire Web publisher and Arthur's marshmallow mentor, noticed, but he replaced his own troubled expression with a genuine smile before his former chauffeur approached.

"Congratulations, Arthur," Jonathan said as he pulled an envelope out of his perfectly tailored, summer-weight wool suit, "on finishing college, landing a great job and becoming a role model for the marshmallow principle and the rewards of delayed gratification. The crowd really seemed inspired by your speech."

"Gee, Mr. P, it should've been you up there on the podium. You're *my* role model, and I never would have gone to college if it hadn't been for your wisdom and generosity." Arthur embraced Jonathan and added, "You're the real marshmallow hero. Lately I feel like a fra—"

"Hey, Arthur, Marshmallow Man!" shouted a graduate who was at least a foot too tall for his gown. "Look at how many marshmallows I caught in my cap. I'm going to put them in a jar on my desk to remind me of my goal to save twenty percent of my paycheck until I have enough for a down payment on a house."

Arthur acknowledged the student and the nearly overflowing mortarboard with a high five. Before he could comment or introduce the man to Jonathan Patient, he was interrupted by a group of well-wishers.

"I'll never forget you, Arthur," said Esther Kim, who'd dyed her hair to match the orange in her gown. "I was ready to quit college and blow my student loan money on a set of drums after I flunked out of freshman math. But then you asked me what I wanted to do with my life, which was to become a veterinarian, and you convinced me that buying the drums would be eating my marshmallows—and maybe illegal—and showed me how to stay focused on my goals. Thanks to you, I have a *scholarship* to one of the best veterinary medicine schools in the country."

"That's just great, Esther. And you'll love Colorado."

Arthur hugged the woman a little harder than he intended when a six-foot-something man slapped him on the back.

"Great speech, Marshy," said Ed Rodriguez, a tanned, muscular graduate whose opened gown revealed the shorts and T-shirt he was wearing. "And my dad says to tell you 'thank you.' He's real relieved he doesn't have to support a beach bum for the rest of his life."

In response to Jonathan Patient's raised eyebrow, but without waiting for an introduction, the young man explained: "Back when Arthur and I met, I was a college misfit—a surfer dude and an accounting geek. I kept skipping class to ride the waves. I got okay grades—all that number stuff comes easy to me—but I never wanted to become a CPA like my dad wanted me to. Then Arthur taught me the marshmallow principle, and I figured out a way to combine my passion for surfing with my talent for accounting. Next week, I start an internship with the CFO of a major surfboard company. I'm actually going to get *paid* to go surfing—it's one of the perks of the job, if you can believe it."

"It sounds as if resisting your marshmallows has really paid off," said Jonathan. "Congratulations, young man. You and your father must both be proud of your accomplishments."

"Yeah, thanks. You must be really, really proud of your son."

"Mr. P's not my fa—" Arthur started to explain, but his attempts were overridden by an onslaught of shouted, sometimes tearful messages of appreciation for the Marshmallow Man and congratulations to the One Hundred Thousand Dollar Man, a nickname bestowed upon Arthur by those who'd heard about his lucrative starting salary at his postgraduation job. Arthur shrugged an apology to Mr. P and tried to share his friends' excitement. But each backslap and hug reminded him that maybe, probably—*absolutely*—he'd gone too far in promoting himself as the marshmallow master.

Yes, he'd accomplished a lot in the last five years. He'd gone from an underachieving, overspending limo driver, whose only measurable talent had been to complete the *New York Times* crossword puzzle every day, to a money-saving, time-savoring college graduate who'd been wined and dined by recruiters from several high-powered firms. And he'd carefully considered each offer before choosing the second-highest paying but most promising position at SlowDown! Inc., a company designed to help the technically *un*savvy cope in a high-higher-highest-speed world. For the past sixty months, Arthur could honestly say he'd been an exemplary marshmallow-resister.

But the last thirty days? Arthur was embarrassed to admit, even to himself, how many marshmallows he'd gobbled since signing on with SlowDown! The marshmallow-from-the-sky stunt alone probably set him back a few thousand dollars (Arthur didn't look at the charge-card slip before signing it, so all he knew for certain was that he hadn't exceeded his fifteen thousand dollar line of credit).

It was a good thing he'd be starting his job in the sales department on Monday. If the company paid him on Fridays the way Mr. P had, he'd be okay, he reasoned, since his rent and car payments weren't due for a couple weeks. And he'd gotten great "No money down" deals on the furniture, appliances and entertainment system he'd purchased for his new place. So everything would work out, right? *Right?* "Ri-i-i-ight?"

"Is what right, Arthur?" asked Amy Jones, one of his many admirers, a woman who'd majored in bed-hopping and beer-guzzling before Arthur's counseling convinced her to pursue a more profitable passion for Chinese language and culture, which, combined with a business degree, had made her the University of Miami's most coveted graduate.

Arthur, who hadn't realized he'd spoken out loud (or completely zoned out), quickly covered his mistake.

"I meant, 'All right!' I hear you're packing your bags for Hong Kong. What a great opportunity. It should be great fun."

"Fun, but not too much fun. Thanks to you, Arthur, I've curbed my party-girl ways. But my job description includes introducing American executives to the city's nightlife. So I'll have a paid excuse to visit the hottest clubs."

"Maybe you'll run into Mr. P at one of them," Arthur said, introducing Amy to his mentor. "He travels all over—Seoul, Taipei, Paris, London, Beijing, Buenos Aires, Brasília, Bogotá, Panama and just about everywhere—so he's bound to be in Hong Kong one of these days."

"You're the famous Mr. P? Well, famous billionaire to most of the world," Amy amended. "But around here you're the amazing marshmallow guy—part of the original Stanford University study, right? And the person Arthur quotes at least ten times a day. I guess I have you as well as Arthur to thank for helping me reach goals more important than finding a hangover cure, which I did, by the way. It's this wild new concept called abstinence."

"I'm glad you learned how to set—and meet—goals important to your success," Jonathan said, "and you're welcome for whatever help I gave you. I'll assume, given your exciting career prospects, that Arthur didn't misquote me."

"Never, Mr. P," Arthur said. "I remember every marshmallow-resisting story you ever told me, practically word for word. I just showed my classmates how to apply your business lessons to our school life."

"And now we have to figure out how to apply your business lessons to *our* business life," Amy said, "but I guess that should be easy, right?"

"Nothing important is ever easy, at least not in my experience," Jonathan said. "And any time you're in a new situation, it's easy to fall into old, often detrimental patterns."

Arthur gulped twice before asking, "What do you mean, Mr. P?"

"Well, a classic example is the advice given to recovering addicts. They're told not to start a job or a relationship until they've been sober for a certain number of months or years. The risk of relapse under stressful situations is great."

"Does that mean that us marshmallow-resisting new-bies shouldn't get jobs now? Are we all supposed to just keep going to school until we get our Master of Marshmallow degree?" Amy asked.

"No, of course not," Jonathan said. "But be careful. Any time you go through a transition, it's easy to regress to more comfortable, longer-practiced habits. So, Amy, you'll want to avoid returning to your overindulging ways. Heed the early warning signs that you may be regressing and get back to marshmallow basics to get you back on track."

"What kind of signs should she look for?" Arthur asked.

"I don't know Amy well enough to make that kind of assessment. But I have one for you, Arthur."

Arthur waited silently for an explanation.

"If you remember, on the last day you worked for me, the day you told me you were going to college, I told you it was time for you to start calling me Jonathan. For four years, that's the name you've greeted me with when we talked by phone or you came by the house for dinner. But today, you addressed me as Mr. P, just as you did when you drove me around town."

"Gee Mr.—uh, Jonathan, that seems pretty trivial. Do you really think I lost my marshmallow mojo just because I called you Mr. P?"

"All I said, Arthur, is that it's a sign. Only you can

decide what it means. Keep practicing what you preached in your commencement speech today, and you'll never eat your marshmallows too soon. But, if you get into trouble, you'll find something of value in that envelope I gave you."

"What envelope? Oh," said Arthur, finally noticing the white rectangle in his hand. "Thank you . . . Jonathan. When did you—? Oh, never mind. Thank you. Should I open it now?"

"Open it one year from today or whenever you feel you're losing your—as you call it—marshmallow mojo, whichever comes first."

Arthur probably should have ripped it open then—or three weeks ago if he'd had it. Instead, he carried it unopened to his car and set the envelope and his cap on the seat of his new BMW convertible. Soon he was heading east on SR 836 toward his ocean-view apartment and away from his anxious thoughts.

He was smiling and singing along with the radio when he merged onto I-95. Perhaps it was the change of direction or the pull of a semitruck passing on his left, but without warning, Arthur's graduation cap flipped over and the envelope beneath it sailed out. From his rearview mirror, Arthur saw the envelope slap against a van advertising fraud protection before it was carried off beyond his vision.

Arthur moaned.

I'm a marshmallow fraud! That's what I was trying to tell Mr. P—Mr. Patient—Jonathan—before we got interrupted. And then I tried to pretend that everything was okay and that I didn't believe in his silly warning signs. Now I've lost his gift, which smacked into a fraud protection ad, and I'm still calling him Mr. P. How many more signs do I need?

Just then a green miniature marshmallow hit him in the head.

2

Marshmallow Madness

T wo Saturdays later, Arthur was sitting in his office—*his* office!—and enjoying renewed confidence. He'd won his modest but coveted four-walls-and-a-door space during the sales training sessions by solving the Migraine Riddle faster than any of his peers. Thanks to his fifty-point answer, Arthur had been the only new hire at SlowDown! to escape assignment to a cubicle in the loud, echo-filled floor space on the eighteenth floor of the company's downtown Miami headquarters.

Arthur heard little noise coming from the floor this morning. He was surprised that so few salespeople—particularly the new ones like him—were working during the weekend, but he was grateful for the quiet opportunity to review lessons learned and ponder how to apply them to his new career.

The Migraine Riddle, for example.

•   •   •

"What would you do," the seminar leader had asked earlier in the week, "if you had access to pills that would relieve a migraine headache in three minutes but no one wanted to buy them because you were selling each two-pill dose for fifty dollars?"

"Reduce the price!" shouted someone in the back.

"Good thing I can't see you or I'd fire you for that very expensive answer," the seminar leader joked. "Let me clarify the conditions. You *must* sell the medicine for fifty dollars or someone else will get the rights to the miracle pills. What do you do?"

More anonymous replies followed: "Advertise!" "Conduct market research!" "Obtain testimonials!" "Get celebrity endorsements!"

Arthur raised his hand and quietly said, "Create the headache."

The seminar leader smiled. "Can you repeat that, Arthur?"

"You have to create the migraine headache. No one who is feeling fine needs medicine, and a person with a normal headache won't spend more than ten dollars on a hundred Tylenol tablets and, personally, I'd buy the generic for half that price," Arthur began. "But someone in the middle of a migraine headache, someone who'd been lying in the dark for two days, someone who couldn't tolerate the slightest noise—let alone the cacophony in this room—without feeling agonizing pain, would happily pay fifty or even a hundred dollars for those pills."

"So are you saying you have to sell to people in the throes of serious migraines?" the seminar leader prompted.

"Well, those are easy sales. Those people will come crawling to your door. But if you want to get the harder, bigger sales, you have to create the headaches. A plumber doesn't have to drum up emergency business—someone whose living room is flooded with bathroom water can't afford to question the cost of getting his pipes fixed. But the same plumber can increase his business if he can create the plumbing emergency in the minds of his customers. He creates the headache before he sells the magic pills."

"And how can you apply that lesson to what we do here at SlowDown!?"

"Well, we can wait for clients to come to us with their technological nightmares or we can pursue them—and land consulting contracts—by creating a need for our services."

•　•　•

Create the headache and then sell the aspirin, that is the most important lesson in the world of sales, thought Arthur as he stared at a foot-high stack of SlowDown! manuals and reports. *Now I have to figure out how to turn that smart answer into smart results. The key is to ask the right questions so as to find out the client's need. The bigger the need, the bigger the headache. It sure makes sense*

Arthur flipped to the chapter 1 summary, hoping to glean the gist of the material before dealing with the details—a study trick that had served him well in college—and was trying to make sense of a Probing Strategy and Needs Analysis chart when a large figure filled his doorway.

"If you're trying to impress the old man by working weekends, you're wasting your time," said the dark-haired young man. "He's on his aptly named *Do Not Disturb* yacht every Friday night to Monday morning."

"And you would know this how?" asked Arthur pleasantly. No need to match the intruder's rudeness—at least until he found out who he was.

"Because he's *my* old man."

"You're Charlie Slow's son? You're Bryan?"

"Uh, yeah. How did you know?"

"I read his bio," Arthur said, pointing to the books on his desk. "Looks like you got his height but not his hair. Do you play ball?"

"No."

"Golf?"

"No."

"Tennis?"

"No." Bryan hesitated a moment, then asked, "Why?"

"They're pastimes mentioned in your dad's bio. I thought—"

"No."

"So you don't—"

"No."

Is this supposed to be part 2 of the Migraine Riddle? Arthur mused, *This kid is giving me a headache.* He decided to end it as painlessly as possible. He rose from his desk, strode toward the door and extended his hand.

"Well, it was nice meeting you, Bryan. I'm Arthur, by the way."

"I know." Bryan ignored the offered handshake, headed for Arthur's desk and slid into the chair behind it before Arthur had a chance to turn around and return his hand to his side.

"You might as well put your feet up," Arthur said. Bryan glared in reply.

"Suit yourself," Arthur said, taking an opposite seat and propping his own feet on the desk. "But I like to be comfortable when engaged in activities I don't enjoy."

Bryan continued his seemingly well-practiced stare-

and-glare routine for more than a minute before Arthur chose to end the impasse.

"You said you knew my name before I introduced myself," Arthur said. "And you knew where my office was located. So I'm guessing you came to my office on purpose but at a time you hoped I wouldn't be here. You could leave a note, hope I'd ignore it and tell whoever sent you that you'd given it your best shot. Am I right?"

"You should have a refrigerator in here," Bryan said.

"Excuse me?" This disjointed conversation was making Arthur feel like he'd wandered into Alice's Wonderland.

"And some magnets. That way you could post all these insipid feel-good quotes"—he waved his hand at the framed quotes that adorned Arthur's office—"where they belong and save your wall space for something important—like cheap poster prints and copies of your diploma the way everyone else does."

"Okay, enough," Arthur said, rising from his chair and leaning over his desk. "First, leave my chair. Then, either explain your purpose—without rude remarks or sarcasm—or leave my office. You're not nearly as clever as you think you are."

" 'We're all mad here. I'm mad. You're mad,' " replied Bryan. Apparently he was on Arthur's wavelength—now he was making Wonderland references too.

" 'How do you know I'm mad?' " continued Arthur.

" 'You must be or you wouldn't have come here,' " Bryan said. "Or at least that's what the Cat told Alice."

"What you lack in social graces, you make up for in intelligence. You seem pretty smart."

"Yeah," said Bryan, suddenly deflated. "That's the problem. I'm *too* smart."

"That's an unusual problem," Arthur said. "But I'm willing to listen to an explanation and help if I can—*if* you stop talking gibberish *and* you don't make fun of my wall hangings. Deal?"

Bryan sighed as he rose from Arthur's seat, walked around the desk and slumped into a chair on the visitor's side. "Deal."

Arthur took a seat next to him and waited. Bryan fidgeted briefly, then spoke in a sudden rush.

"The problem started a month ago when my mother opened my mail—my test scores on the SAT—and now she wants to ruin my life."

"Was she disappointed in your scores?"

"Worse! Just the opposite. I was always an average student, got unremarkable grades and my parents didn't interfere. But then I got this freakishly high score on the SATs, and my mom's insisting I go to Harvard. Harvard! Do you have any idea how horrible that would be?"

"No. For many students, going to Harvard would be a dream, not a nightmare. Why don't you want to go?"

"Because it would ruin my plans," Bryan whined. "I'm in a band—a serious band, so don't laugh—and we're saving money from our local gigs so we can hit the road next summer. I can't be wasting my time in some Ivy League nerd school when I could be rockin' my way to Hollywood and a big recording contract."

"Maybe you won't get in," Arthur offered helpfully. "Even with great scores, a lot of students get rejected from Harvard."

"Not the ones they recruit!" Bryan moaned. "They came to my school and pulled me and two science geeks out of class and offered each of us admission. Then the principal announced it over the intercom. I was mortified. It completely ruined my reputation. Someone changed the name on my locker to Brayn!"

Arthur remained quiet for a moment. He was having a hard time understanding—much less sympathizing with Bryan the Brayn's plight. Here was the son of a very wealthy businessman, bright enough to be wooed by Harvard despite his best efforts to be a mediocre student, and he gripes that he doesn't want to go? Well, boo hoo to him! But maybe there was more to the story. Arthur decided to find out.

"Let's back this conversation up a bit," Arthur said. "Who sent you to see me and why?"

"My parents . . . and I don't know why. To convince

me to go to Harvard, I guess. They said something about marshmallows . . ."

"Well, maybe they sent you to the wrong person. I won't convince you to go to Harvard—or to do anything else you don't want to do."

"You won't?" Bryan sat up a few degrees straighter in his chair and displayed the promise of a smile.

"No. That would be a waste of my time and yours. But what I can do is help you determine whether it's in *your* best interests to go and, if not, show you how to devise an alternate plan to attain your goals. Are you serious enough about becoming a rock star to listen?"

"Well, I like the part about not going to Harvard," Bryan said. "And, of course, I'm serious about becoming a rock *super*star. So, yeah, I'm interested." Bryan shifted slightly upward in his chair again.

"Good, so tell me, what kind of musician are you?"

"Guitarist. Lead guitarist in our band."

"Do you play any other instruments?"

"No."

"Do you sing?"

"Backup. Lead a few times when our vocalist got sick. But usually just backup, which is cool. Guitar's my thing. It will *always* be my thing."

"Okay, now I'll ask you a question."

"Isn't that all you've been doing?"

"Fair enough," Arthur replied without rancor. He was enjoying himself now. "I'll ask you a different kind of question: if your father gave you ten thousand dollars to spend any way you wanted to further your guitar career, how would you spend it?"

"That's easy. I'd buy a Gibson Les Paul custom guitar or maybe a 1960s Fender."

"And what would you do with the rest of the money?"

Bryan snorted. "What *rest*? I'd be lucky to get either of those for a penny under ten grand. I'd probably have to spend my savings on top of that for a vintage Fender."

"And would you?"

"Hel—heck, yes! Those guitars are awesome. Jimi Hendrix played a Stratocaster; Eric Clapton has a Fender named after him."

"Well, that's your problem," Arthur said. "You're a marshmallow-eater."

"Huh?"

"If you spent a gift of ten thousand dollars and your life savings on a guitar, you'd be eating all of your marshmallows and doing *nothing* to get you closer to becoming a rock star."

"But, but—"

"I know. Hendrix and Clapton are among the world's greatest guitarists. *Rolling Stone* says so. And Fender and

Gibson make terrific guitars. So do Gretsch, Epiphone and other companies I've never heard of. But it's not expensive equipment that made these guys great. I don't know Clapton's history, but I'm a Hendrix fan, and I know he practiced on a broomstick before his dad gave him a used ukulele, and I don't believe he even owned a real guitar by the time he was your age. Do you own a guitar?"

"Of course! Three actually. My dad's old acoustic, a vintage Gibson made out of Brazilian rosewood. My first electric, a top-of-the-line Yamaha, and an awesome Fender I got for my sixteenth birthday." Bryan sighed. "Okay, I can see why I don't actually *need* another guitar. But if you were giving me ten thousand dollars, why shouldn't I have one? And what does it have to do with marshmallows?"

"Trust me, I'd have blown all my money on the guitar too when I was your age. I spent my entire college fund on a car just to impress girls. I couldn't even blame talent on my decision, just hormones." Arthur smiled. "It was a decision that kept me trapped in a self-defeating lifestyle until Jonathan Patient, my boss at the time, told me about the marshmallow theory."

"All right, you've got my attention," Bryan said, removing all traces of a slouch from his posture. "If a billionaire believes there's a lesson to be learned from marshmallows, then maybe I should too."

Arthur explained to Bryan that Mr. Patient had been a participant in a Stanford University study in which pre-school children were left alone in a room with a marsh-mallow for fifteen minutes. "They were told that if they didn't eat the marshmallow, they would be rewarded with a second marshmallow. For a four year old to wait fifteen minutes would be the equivalent of telling an adult to wait two hours for a cup of coffee—no easy task. Fourteen or so years later, when the kids from the study were in col-lege, the experimenters followed up to see if the children who resisted the marshmallows had turned out any differ-ently than the ones who had eaten theirs right away."

"And did they?" Bryan asked.

"Yes! It turned out that kids who didn't eat the marsh-mallow—and those who resisted the longest—did better in school, got along better with others and managed stress better than the children who ate the first marshmallow shortly after the adult left the room. They also did re-markably better on their college entrance exams, scoring an average of two hundred and ten points higher on the SAT. The marshmallow-resisters turned out to be vastly more successful than the marshmallow-eaters."

"That's interesting," Bryan began, "but what does that have to do with my buying or not buying the guitar or going or not going to Harvard?"

"Your instinct was to spend the entire ten thousand

dollars on something you wanted *now* without even thinking about whether that money might serve a better long-term purpose. People who can delay gratification— not eat a marshmallow or spend money instantly—have a far greater chance of being successful than those who seek immediate rewards. There is an eternal battle be- tween impulse and restraint, wanting things and having the discipline to say no, getting everything now or wait- ing for the right moment when you can have a lot more. You might not see it now my friend, but there is perhaps no psychological skill more profound than the willpower to resist an impulse."

"So you're saying it would be stupid to spend ten thousand dollars on a guitar?"

"No, I'm suggesting that if you've been given ten thou- sand dollars to boost your career, you should seek the best value for your money, not merely satisfy an immediate de- sire. You need more than an instrument to succeed as a musi- cian. What if, on the day you picked up your Les Paul guitar, you're offered a gig in Los Angeles? How would you afford to get there? To eat? To buy new strings for the guitar?"

"I'd ask my dad—"

"He gave you ten thousand dollars yesterday, and be- sides, when will you stop asking your daddy for stuff and start accepting responsibility?"

"Oh, I see."

"So how'd you feel if you and your fancy new guitar had to stay home and miss the L.A. opportunity?"

"Like I had a really bad case of marshmallow poisoning."

"You'd feel sick all right!" Arthur laughed. "Now, if you want to learn how to apply the marshmallow theory to your goal of becoming a rock star and to whether attending Harvard might benefit you as well as please your parents, you're going to have to spend some time with my 'insipid feel-good quotes.'"

"You didn't mock me when I said I wanted to become a rock star—most people do—so I guess I shouldn't make fun of whatever's important to you," Bryan said. "But you've got a ton of reading material on your walls. Where do I start?"

"At the beginning," Arthur said, handing Bryan a pad of paper and a pen and pointing to a sign he'd created nearly five years ago, while he was still living at the coach house at the Patient estate, and since refined:

THE SIX-STEP MARSHMALLOW PLAN TO SWEET SUCCESS IN ANYTHING—AND EVERYTHING!

1. **What do you need to change?**
   What are you doing now that is helping you in your life? What will you commit to changing?

2. **What are your strengths and weaknesses?**

    What do you need to improve and how can you best make these improvements?

3. **What are your major goals?**

    Pick at least five and write them down. They must be measurable and have a deadline. If you can't see a goal, you can't achieve it.

4. **What is your plan?**

    How are you going to achieve your goals? What strategies do you have to implement right now to stop eating your marshmallows?

5. **What are you going to do to put your plan into action?**

    What will you commit to doing today, tomorrow, next week, next year to help you reach your goals?

6. **Persevere.**

    Don't give up. If you fall down seven times, get up eight. The marshmallow principle works. Enjoy the challenge as well as the rewards of delayed gratification.

Bryan completed the list and looked balefully at Arthur. "Now what? This looks like a lot of work. How is it going to help?"

"Yes, you're right. Planning and achieving your goals does take a lot of work. But I can help you simplify it, so let's schedule an appointment for you to meet me here at the same time next week. Ponder the questions, answer the ones you can, and we'll discuss it in greater detail next Saturday."

"Next Saturday?"

"Yes, does that work for you?"

"I guess so," Bryan grumbled. "But still, how does all this list-making help? I already know what I want to do."

"We'll discuss that more next week too. But remember when Alice asked the Cat for directions to 'somewhere'?"

"Yeah," Bryan answered. "The Cat told her it didn't matter which way she traveled, she was certain to end up somewhere 'if only you walk long enough.'"

"Yes," Arthur said. "And a few minutes ago, you said you planned to 'hit the road' to launch your music career. If you don't give more thought to your destination—your real goals—the 'somewhere' you end up may be a long way from rock stardom."

"You mean like Harvard?"

"Maybe," Arthur said. "But you never know. When you start seriously focusing on your goals, you may discover that Harvard's on the map to getting there."

Bryan started to twist his mouth into a scowl, but reshaped it into a half grin before turning to leave, waving his copy of The Six-Step Marshmallow Plan to Sweet Success over his head in a good-bye gesture. *No sense arguing with Arthur now,* he thought. *I'll prove him wrong with his marshmallow make-work. I'll marshmallow myself as far away from Harvard as possible!*

*   *   *

Arthur returned with enthusiasm to the stack of study materials on his desk. He looked forward to mentoring the boss's son. It never hurt to get in good with the powers that be, and he welcomed the chance to continue the marshmallow mentoring he'd enjoyed so much in school. Besides, concentrating on other people's needs helped him avoid worrying about his own. Maybe, he told himself, the problems of his mounting bills and the missing envelope—his graduation gift from Mr. P—will get resolved without any effort on his part.

Maybe. But perhaps Arthur was slipping deeper down the rabbit hole into magical thinking and marshmallow mayhem.

3

Stressed— and Stretched— to Impress

Again and again and *again*, Arthur checked his online bank account statement to see if his first direct deposit from SlowDown! had registered. It was his third Friday on the job—he'd never had to work so long without getting paid before—but he knew the thrill of his biggest paycheck ever would be worth the wait. Sometime today, based on his calculations, his account would grow by five thousand dollars! But when?

The fingers on his right hand were growing numb from the repeated mouse clicking, and Arthur idly wondered whether his health insurance plan covered carpal tunnel syndrome treatments. After the next log-in and before the subsequent letdown, a loud distraction interrupted him.

"What is *wrong* with you?" shouted a short, dark-haired woman wearing an old-money outfit and a newly angered attitude. "What. Is. Wrong. With. You?"

"My hand hurts a little," Arthur offered, but instantly regretted his attempt at humor when a tiny shaking fist nearly connected with his nose as he rose to his feet. "I'm sorry. How may I help you?"

"It was all my husband's idea. He said you and some marshmallow theory would talk some sense into my son. Instead you tell him to skip Harvard, tune his guitar and run off to Hollywood!"

"Hello, uh, Mrs. Slow?" Arthur asked and waited for a nodded reply for continuing in what he hoped would be job-saving reasonableness. "Perhaps Bryan misunderstood me, but I never told him not to go to Harvard and I certainly didn't tell him to run off to Hollywood. I just gave him some tools to help him shape and make intelligent, focused decisions about his long-term goals."

"The only intelligent decision he needs to make is to accept Harvard's offer, and he needs to do it in the very short term or they'll give his slot to someone else," Mrs. Slow said. "Instead, he's spending all of his time budgeting a road trip to California, and he says it's what you told him to do. I want you to start talking some sense into him or stop talking to him—period. Do you understand?"

What Arthur understood is that he was in trouble. An angry boss's spouse could be more dangerous to his career than an angry boss. What could he *truthfully* say to Mrs. Slow that would satisfy her? Arthur took a deep breath and pointed to the opposite wall.

"Mrs. Slow, everything Bryan and I talked about, everything I advised about began and ended with what's written on the wall over there," Arthur said.

"What wall and what writing?" Mrs. Slow asked derisively. "It looks like you made wallpaper out of a book of affirmations or something."

"Those were Bryan's sentiments, somewhat differently expressed," Arthur said. "But after I told him about the rewards of delayed gratification, he seemed genuinely interested in The Six-Step Marshmallow Plan to Sweet Success in Anything—and Everything! He copied it down, took it home and promised to address the questions before we met again. We didn't discuss the plan in detail, but if you'd like, I could go over it with you. Maybe it would help you understand—"

"Understand what? I don't need to understand anything. Bryan should go to Harvard, period."

"Maybe it would help you understand," Arthur repeated, "your goal of Bryan going to Harvard—why it's important to you." Arthur took a deep breath and asked, "Why is it important to you?"

"Why? Because I want the best for Bryan. I want him to be successful and happy—what every mother wants for her child. And Harvard will make him a success."

"If you believe that, take a look at the first question: What do you need to change? What do you need to change, Mrs. Slow, to achieve your goal of Bryan finding success and happiness at Harvard?"

"Change? Why do I need to change anything? This is about my son, not about me," Mrs. Slow said.

"If attending Harvard was Bryan's goal, we wouldn't be having this discussion," Arthur countered. "Harvard is *your* goal, and short of forcing Bryan to go there—which would be eating your marshmallows—you need to change your strategy." Arthur was tempted to add, *"Or change your mind about Harvard,"* but he wasn't prepared to be that direct with the president's wife—certainly not before his first paycheck.

"What's wrong with forcing him to go? It would be for his own good."

"Possibly. It could turn out to be his pile of bricks!" Arthur said.

"Bricks?"

"After talking to Bryan last week, I did some research about musicians. I hoped to impress him with a long list of rock stars who graduated from an Ivy League or other great school, including my alma mater, the University of Miami. I'm still working on the list, but I came across a story about Will Smith that I thought he'd enjoy."

"Are you talking about Will Smith, the actor, that *Hitch* guy?" Mrs. Slow asked.

"Yes, he's also a Grammy Award–winning rapper who was nominated for an Oscar and Golden Globe awards for his roles in *Ali* and *The Pursuit of Happyness* and whose movies regularly top the box-office charts."

"Did he go to Harvard?" Mrs. Slow asked, her expression hopeful for the first time.

"No, he turned down an offer to M.I.T., but—"

"He didn't go to *any* university?" Mrs. Slow sneered. "Why do I want to hear about him?"

Bryan got his height from his dad, but his dark hair—and dark attitude—are definitely gifts from his mother. I'd hate to be locked in a room with the two of them, Arthur thought to himself before replying.

"Because Will Smith is extremely successful and, by all accounts, happy—just what you want for Bryan," Arthur said. "And the brick wall story demonstrates the sixth step to marshmallow success—perseverance."

"Okay, I'm listening," Mrs. Slow said.

"Will Smith's father, who owned a refrigerator business in Philadelphia, tore down a brick wall of his ice house and told Will and his brother to rebuild it. The wall was fifty feet long and fourteen feet high. Will didn't believe he'd see the project—what he called the Great Wall of Philly—completed in his lifetime.

"It took more than half a year, but the Smith brothers finally built the wall. Guess what the father said?" Arthur asked Mrs. Slow.

"Good job?"

"What he said was, 'Now, don't ever tell me there's anything you can't do.' And Will learned an important lesson, which he revealed in *Premiere* magazine. He said of his dad:

" 'He'd been waiting six months just to deliver that line. And I got it, there's nothing insurmountable if you just keep laying the bricks, you know? You go one brick at a time and eventually there will be a wall. You can't avoid it. So I don't worry much about walls. I just concentrate on the bricks, and the walls take care of themselves.' "

"Well, that's it then," Mrs. Slow said with a victorious smile. "I will force my son to go to Harvard and, someday, like Will Smith, he'll thank me for it in a magazine."

"That wasn't the point of the story. It was about believing in and working toward *your* dreams, not about imposing them on someone else. I really think—"

But Mrs. Slow was already making a rapid exit out of

Arthur's office. She'd gotten what she wanted out of the meeting even if it wasn't what she needed.

And now she's going to take the Will Smith marshmallow I gave her and shove it down Bryan's throat. He'll blame me for her manipulative efforts and when they fail—and they will!—she'll blame me too.

Arthur sighed, turned his attention back to his computer and refreshed his banking site's home page, certain that evidence of a fat paycheck would improve his mood. He retyped his password, hit the Enter key and watched as his direct deposit from SlowDown! appeared. He logged out and loped toward the elevator that would take him to the payroll department, but retreated to his office when he heard his desk phone ring.

"Hey, Arthur," said a familiar voice. "We're waiting for you here at Study Break to celebrate your payday. And remember, lunch is on you."

"I'm on my way," Arthur said, although he had, in fact, forgotten about the party and his role as *paying* host. But he wasn't about to admit that lapse (or far worse mistakes). So instead he boasted his way to another expensive error in judgment. "Order everyone at the table some appetizers and buy everyone in the restaurant a round of drinks from the University of Miami's most successful new graduate—and make it two rounds if it takes me more than twenty minutes to get there."

Thirty-one minutes later, Arthur pulled into the parking lot of his favorite university hangout. He circled twice before finding a remote spot next to a Dumpster. Arthur counted cars on his way to the restaurant's front entrance and moaned. If his very modest estimates about the number of patrons and the cost of tequila and nachos were correct, Arthur had already blown his first paycheck. What would be left of his second, unearned paycheck by the time this "celebration" concluded? Arthur would save a little money, at least. His own appetite was ruined.

4

The Fall from Marshmallow Grace

"Come, on, Arthur. Just one more story. Who knows when we'll get together like this again? It's not like we can just go knocking on your door any time we want the way we did in college. So give us just one more shot of wisdom before you leave. Pleeeeeease?"

"Okay." Arthur grumbled good-naturedly in reply to his pals who were crowded into the Study Break Grill's largest booth. "But no more shots of anything else, and since this is a story about cookies, it will have to substitute for dessert too. So what will it be? Another story or a slice of key lime pie?"

"No pie?" The chorus of slightly inebriated groans

and giggles echoed loudly enough to merit disapproving stares from other diners. Arthur motioned for the group to be quiet, then offered to sweeten the chocolate chip story deal. "Since the cookie story doesn't originate with me—I think it's one Stephen Covey tells in *The Seven Habits of Highly Effective People*—I'll include a second, very personal story about making a mistake that could get me fired!"

Arthur now had his friends' complete, *silent* attention and interested looks from some of the recently irritated patrons as well.

"A woman waiting for her flight to board purchased a book and a box of cookies and sat down next to a man in the waiting area," Arthur began. "As she read her book, she extended her arm and grabbed a cookie from the center of the table. From the corner of her eye, she saw the gentleman helping himself to a cookie as well. She couldn't believe the nerve of the man but didn't say anything.

"She continued reading and reached for another cookie. Again the man took one too. The woman was furious—how dare the man invite himself to take her cookies and invade her personal space? Still she kept silent—she didn't want to make a scene and find herself the subject of some new airline security measure. So she and the man both kept helping themselves to the box of cookies until, finally, the man shared the last cookie with her by breaking it in half and handing her a piece. Then the man stood, bowed, smiled and told the woman to have a wonderful day before leaving to board his flight.

"By now the woman was furious and might have risked the consequences of shouting a cookie-crumbling insult at him, but her own flight was called. She gathered her book and reached for her carry-on bag only to discover that *her* box of cookies was tucked, unopened, into an outside pouch."

Amid appreciative laughter, Esther, the future veterinarian whose normally black hair still bore traces of graduation-day orange, asked, "Great story, Arthur, but what does it mean and how does it relate to your story about possibly getting fired? Did you get into a cookie-snatching fight at work?"

"I did something a lot worse," Arthur admitted, "but let me explain the cookie story first: the woman and the man at the airport shared the same experience, but not only were her assumptions incorrect, her attitude was selfish and angry. The man, who had greater cause to be disturbed, was instead polite and gracious. Each of us at this table, and probably many people in the restaurant, is going through a period of change in which our paradigms—our accepted patterns and beliefs—may also have to shift if we want to be successful. We all have to remember that a paradigm is a map, not the actual territory. It is an interpretation of reality but not reality itself, so we must change our paradigms because a lot of what we have learned or have been taught might not be totally true."

"So what happened to you, Arthur, to put your career in jeopardy in less than a month?" Ed, the surfing CPA, asked.

"A few minutes ago you traded dessert for another story because you recognized that we can no longer meet at any and all hours to chat, that you can no longer knock on my door whenever you feel like it because our circumstances and locations are changing, right?" Arthur paused to accept a round of quizzical nods, then shared his recent experience with Bryan Slow and his mother.

"I made the mistake of treating them the way I treated you throughout college. I gave both of them incomplete advice, expecting that they'd naturally come back begging the Marshmallow Man for additional help, that I could teach them the theory of delayed gratification a snippet at a time, the way I shared it with you, the way Jonathan Patient shared it with me.

"But each of you came to me voluntarily—Bryan was forced. And neither Bryan nor his mother has reason ever to speak to me again—by family extension, they're my bosses—and each left my office thinking I'd sided with the other about Harvard and music. I've lost their trust and respect—if I had ever even gained them—and I could lose my job over my stupid arrogance."

"But you won't, will you, Arthur?" Esther asked. "You'll make the shift in your attitude, change whatever needs to be changed, and succeed as both a salesman and a delayed gratification expert at SlowDown!"

"Of course!" Arthur said with forced bravado. "But don't ask me yet about my plan—I just fully came to understand my plight during this lunch. How about you ask me again in a month? We should meet before you take off to Colorado, Esther, and the rest of us get too busy with disparate schedules. As we're all learning—maybe me especially—our world is changing and we need to change or risk falling off the planet. Or maybe into its cracks. Or something bad globally—I've lost myself in the science metaphor."

"Don't worry, Arthur. We understand you, even if you and your bosses don't," said Esther.

The group exchanged hugs, handshakes and promises to get together in four weeks. Arthur rose to leave but sat back down when his waitress tapped him on the shoulder.

"Can you spare me a couple minutes of genius after your friends leave?" asked Akilah, who'd been serving him food, drinks and sarcasm since his first day as a University of Miami freshman.

"Sure," said Arthur, thankful that his sales job permitted flexible hours and grateful that he'd toasted his pals with shots of espresso, not tequila. He'd be working long into the night to make up for this lengthy luncheon. But he didn't mind stretching it longer for Akilah. Her sharp tongue belied a shortage of self-confidence, and he liked to think their sparring helped boost her esteem. "How can I help?"

Arthur was surprised when Akilah slid into the booth next to him and shocked when she whispered in his ear, "I didn't want to embarrass you in front of your marshmallow groupies, but your credit card was declined."

Arthur blanched. *Did I charge fifteen thousand dollars— my credit limit—to my card in less than a month? Impossible!*

"There must be a mistake—"

"I ran the card three times and called the company directly. You can call them yourself if you want, but—"

"No problem," bluffed Arthur. "I'll work it out with them later." He reached into his wallet and pulled out another piece of plastic. "Here, you can put the meal on this card—and add an extra ten dollars to your tip for your, uh, discretion." Arthur hesitated. "I'm not used to seeing this sensitive side to you, Akilah. What's up with you?"

"What's up with *you?*" Akilah demanded. "You can keep the ten dollars and the rest of your too generous tip and tell me why you, of all people, went over your charge card limit. How does overspending fit into the marshmallow success plan?

"And don't even *think* about putting me off with some lame excuse," Akilah continued. "I just ended my shift, and I've got no place to go, so you're not leaving until I say so." Akilah stretched her legs across to the opposite bench and signaled her shift replacement to the booth.

"Could you please bring us some coffee and pie?" Akilah asked sweetly. Then in a volume loud enough for the dishwashers in the back kitchen to hear, she added, "And put it on my tab. My in-debt customer can't afford key lime today."

"I thought you didn't want to embarrass me," Arthur whispered.

"I said I didn't want to make you look bad in front of *your* friends. Never said I wouldn't ridicule you in front of mine." Akilah laughed in amusement and then sighed in concern. "But I promise to keep my voice and my attitude down if you tell me straight what kind of trouble you're in. And like I said, you're not going anywhere until you do."

Arthur considered. He knew Akilah could keep her pledge—she was a black belt in Tae Kwon Do, the Korean martial art sport. He was certain she could balance a tray of drinks in one hand and toss him out the door with the other. Besides, he could use a sympathetic listener, and he was too proud to confess his recent mistakes to anyone else.

So Arthur told Akilah *almost* everything about his marshmallow meltdown. He told her that ever since he received the job offer from SlowDown!, he'd reverted to his old stressed-to-impress habits, leasing a car and apartment he couldn't afford, buying expensive furniture with "buy now, pay later" options, hiring an airplane pilot for the "special effects" part of his commencement address and treating friends to drinks and meals to show off his One Hundred Thousand Dollar Man status.

"What kind of palace are you living in that you can't handle rent on a salary of eight thousand dollars a month?"

"It's not a palace," Arthur muttered defensively. "It's a two-bedroom condo with a decent ocean view."

"Okay, so that explains two, three thousand dollars and the car is costing you, what? Five hundred dollars? That leaves you five thousand to pay taxes, bills and restaurant tabs." Akilah paused, then asked, "What was the limit on that tapped-out credit card?"

"Fifteen thousand dollars."

"So, you're making eight thousand dollars a month and spending twenty-three thousand? What's going on, Arthur? You can't have that many friends to feed. Are you on drugs? Gambling? Buying female companionship?"

"No, no and don't insult me," Arthur said. "I budget-
ed for the car and apartment and I allowed for credit-card
bills. I'm never going to repeat the marshmallows-from-
the-sky extravagance, so that debt would be manageable
too. It's just that, that . . . that . . ."

"Spit it out, Arthur—and I don't mean the coffee or
the meringue. Tell me what's going on and tell me now or
I'll bar you from ever coming to Study Break again."

"You can't. You wouldn't—"

Akilah waggled Arthur's credit card in the air. "I can
and I would. The management takes a hard line on dead-
beats, and you would have walked out the door without
paying if I hadn't stopped you."

"Akilah!" Arthur protested. "That's not—"

"True? Maybe, maybe not. But I dare you to call my
bluff. How can you be a judge of the truth anyway, Arthur, when all you've been doing since I sat down is stuff-
ing your face with pie and my head with lies?"

"I haven't lied—"

"And you haven't told me the truth either. Your lame
story doesn't add up. You should know better than to try
to confuse a career waitress with faulty math. You're just
a puffed-up marshmallow mess who thought you could
dump your pathetic problems on me because it didn't
matter what I thought. It's not like I'm your client or your
employer or your *friend*."

Akilah suddenly stopped talking and Arthur prepared himself for a second-wind rampage, a first-class beating or third-degree burns. But Akilah didn't yell, hit or fling coffee at Arthur. What she did, instead, shocked him. Akilah started to cry, deep bellowing sobs that rattled the cups on the table and upset Arthur even more. *Why does Akilah care whether I'm a little or a lot overextended or what portion of my salary I owe in rent?*

Akilah ran from the dining room, but before Arthur had a chance to ponder the wisdom of a fast exit, Akilah returned, laboring under the weight of a five-gallon coffee urn. She set it down hard—much harder than necessary—on the table in front of Arthur, who heard a familiar but unexpected ka-ching when it landed.

"Open it, Arthur!" Akilah demanded, her attitude turning from sad to mad. Arthur quickly obeyed and discovered hundreds and hundreds of coins, crumpled bills and some old napkins and food order slips covered with handwritten scrawls. Arthur didn't speak, but his eyes asked the question: *what does this mean?*

"That's every tip you ever gave me, Arthur, from the five quarters you left me during your first week as a freshman and including the two hundred dollars you gave me today." Akilah paused and grinned without humor. "I don't know how much is in there, but I guess I'll find out when I cash them in for blackjack chips in Las Vegas this weekend."

"Vegas? There must be thousands of dollars in there. Why would you save the money all this time just to risk losing it all on a gambling trip? That would be—"

"Eating my marshmallows," Akilah finished for him. "Yeah, I know. But I figure if you're going to gobble all of your marshmallows—your college degree, your career, everything you've worked for—then I figure I might as well wager mine on a deck of cards."

"Please, Akilah, don't do something you'll regret just because you're mad at me. It's amazing that you've saved all that money and—"

"Don't waste your breath talking to me. I've been listening to you *talk* for four years. I even took notes," she said, plucking several pieces of paper from the coffee urn. "I've studied your marshmallow principles," she continued, "the ones about successful people being willing to do what unsuccessful people are not willing to do, how successful people don't break their promises, et cetera, et cetera. And I've memorized your stories about Larry Bird dribbling a ball for hours before a game so he could play around any cracks or faults in the floor. I know about that right-handed second baseman, Jorge Posada, who learned how to become a catcher and a switch-hitter, and ended up with a fifty-one-million-dollar major league contract with the New York Yankees. I could recite, word for word, every story and piece of advice you shared in this room.

Look, I even carry with me the little motivational mini-book you gave me the day we met." Akilah opened her purse and took out the worn little book. She opened it to page 7 and read, "'Rather than acknowledge a mistake, nations have gone to war, families have been separated and individuals have sacrificed everything dear to them. Admitting that you have been wrong is just another way of saying that you are wiser today than yesterday.'

"I listened to you, Arthur, and I believed in you. Because of you, I thought I could reach my goal of owning a restaurant. Now, because of you, I don't believe I'll ever be anything but a lousy waitress. You were my marshmallow hero, Arthur. Now I think you're just a sweet-talking fraud."

"Please, Akilah, don't give up on your goals. I know I've made mistakes and you're right, I haven't admitted or told you the complete truth about all of them. But just because I've gotten off my marshmallow track doesn't mean you should abandon yours." Arthur glanced at his watch and groaned. "Akilah, I really have to get back to work. But if I promise to meet you here in a week and tell you everything, will you promise me that you won't go to Vegas before then?"

"Well, I guess the dealers will be waiting for me no matter when I get there. So I'll wait a week, but not a day longer. And if you don't convince me that your marshmallow theory is more than sugary fluff, I'll be on the next plane to gamble *your* money away."

"Thanks, Akilah. I'm really looking forward to hearing about your restaurant plans and—"

"Save it, Arthur. I don't want to hear another word out of you until next week. And by then, you'd better have plenty to say."

• • •

Arthur kept quiet, and he kept his head down as he headed out of the restaurant toward his car. What a long, horrible day! The confrontation with Mrs. Slow, the letdown of his paycheck—*please let it be a payroll error!*—and the devastating conversation with Akilah. And he still had a long night ahead of him at the office.

Lost in dark, defeating thoughts, Arthur paid no attention to his surroundings. He didn't notice the little girl chasing a helium-filled balloon; he didn't notice a clandestine couple kissing good-bye and he didn't notice an envelope stuck to the side of the Dumpster a foot away from where he'd left his car.

It was an envelope with his name on it, his graduation present from Jonathan Patient, the one that included the secret to restoring his marshmallow mojo.

5

Wages and Wagers

Three days later, on his fourth Monday at work, Arthur felt more discouraged than ever. Bryan had skipped his Saturday meeting, and both he and Mrs. Slow were ignoring his calls. And the details of his paycheck had been confirmed: the $829.62 deposited into his banking account was not a clerical error. The only mistake had been Arthur's, who'd been deceiving himself for weeks about his earnings at SlowDown!

It wasn't entirely his fault. Arthur had never held a corporate job before—he'd been Jonathan Patient's chauffeur for ten years and an independent online rare coin broker while in college—so his knowledge of withholding pay, expense accounts and car allowances was slim. Still, he knew that the sales director who offered him the job had distinguished between base salary and commissions when describing Arthur's six-figure package. But he'd hoped that the distinction would be minor and avoided measuring that wish against reality. He'd enjoyed (and come to believe) the hype of being the One Hundred Thousand Dollar Man.

Now he was forced to face the truth of being an Eight Hundred Dollar Guy, which Betty, the head of payroll, had explained in painful, unavoidable detail:

"We operate on a two-week pay period," she said in a clipped voice that hinted at annoyance, "and you'll always be a pay period behind. Since you started in the middle of a pay cycle, you were paid for one week, even though you've worked three."

Then she added, with a little too much enthusiasm for Arthur's comfort, "But, don't worry, you'll get those two weeks' pay when you leave the company."

"Eight hundred dollars a week would be forty thousand dollars a year," Arthur said, "and I was told I'd be making a hundred thousand. I know there are deductions for taxes—"

"A lot of new hires in sales get confused," Betty interrupted, "between their base pay and their total wage packages. In your case, your biweekly paycheck is based on a salary of sixty thousand dollars. The rest comes from your car allowance, expense account, health care plan and projected commissions.

"So if you do your job well and start *selling*," she continued, "your paycheck will improve accordingly. In the meantime, you can look forward to receiving your car allowance on the thirtieth as well as your expenses, if you submitted them by the fifteenth. Did you?"

"Uh, no, I didn't have any until last week and—"

"Then you'll get those at the end of next month—if you submit your report on time—and, more good news, you'll get a two-thousand-dollar-a-month draw on your commission for each of the next three months to help you out until you start *earning* your commissions, which are paid in the month following the one in which we receive payment from your clients. Understand?"

Arthur didn't comprehend anything except that his pay this month would be 10 percent of what he'd anticipated, but he nodded, thanked Betty for her time and left. After a few woe-is-us discussions with some of the sales staff, Arthur had a better grasp of the details: he'd clear a thousand dollars this month, five thousand the next three and then his income would drop to three thousand dollars a month or less when he had to start paying back the commission draw. Arthur knew he needed to make some big sales fast if he wanted to support his lifestyle before every credit card he owned reached its limit.

•   •   •

He spent the rest of the day pursuing sales leads and trying to reach Bryan and his mother. He contacted twenty-two companies and left four informative but purposely confusing messages on the Slow's answering machine:

"Hey, Bryan, it's Arthur. I missed you Saturday. Wondered if you had any questions about the marshmallow principle and how to apply it to your decision about Harvard and your music career. For what it's worth, I did some research, and I wanted to let you know that going to Harvard won't ruin your chances of becoming a rock star. It's not just future presidents and Nobel Prize winners who go to prestigious schools. Matt Damon, Tommy Lee Jones and Fred Gwynne, of The Munsters, attended Harvard. Henry Winkler graduated from Yale—and who's cooler than the Fonz, right? Brian May, the guitarist who gave us the classic "We Will Rock You," was working on his Ph.D. in astronomy before Queen struck it big. Oh, and almost forgot, Tom Morello, twenty-sixth on Rolling Stone's list of greatest guitarists of all time, spent eight hours a day perfecting his signature style while studying political science at Harvard, graduating from there with honors. Just something for you to think about. Give me a call and let's talk some more."

*   *   *

"Hello, Mrs. Slow. This is Arthur. We talked last week about Bryan, and I feel bad that I wasn't able to finish the story I was telling you about Will Smith. Thought you might want to know why he declined the scholarship from M.I.T. His father made him a deal: Will had a year to prove he was serious about becoming a rap star. If it didn't pan out, he'd enroll full time at M.I.T. As you may recall, the Fresh Prince won a Grammy at age nineteen and went on to win more recognition, including multiple Golden Globe and Oscar nominations. Just thought you'd want to know this since you enjoyed the brick wall story so much. Please call if I can be of any more help. Good-bye, Mrs. Slow."

"Hey, Bryan, it's Arthur again. I've been doing some more research and it turns out that musicians, maybe more than anyone else in the entertainment industry, suffer some serious financial woes. The list of crash-and-burn victims is pretty long: Mick Fleetwood, Toni Braxton, Marvin Gaye, Andy Gibb, Merle Haggard, MC Hammer, Ron Isley, La Toya Jackson, Kacey Jones, Chaka Kahn, Cyndi Lauper, Meat Loaf, Willie Nelson, Wayne Newton and Tammy Wynette all filed for bankruptcy protection at some point. Also Will Smith, who's doing great now, evaded taxes *and nearly went bankrupt after the IRS caught up with him at the peak of his rap career. Maybe if he'd taken some business classes at a good university . . . So how're you coming with that music tour budget? Anyway, just thought you'd find this interesting and helpful in meeting your goals. Bye for now."*

"Hello, Mrs. Slow, Arthur again. Sorry to bother you, but I wanted to help you out in your Harvard discussions with Bryan. If he's telling you that he doesn't need a university degree to become a successful rock star, well, he's right. Of the one hundred most highly acclaimed guitarists in the world, only eight graduated from college, from what I can confirm. Eleven others enrolled in community and four-year schools, but didn't complete their studies. There is one Harvard grad among this prestigious group—you can ask Bryan about him—as well as a law degree recipient and a Ph.D. candidate, but the correlation between Ivy League and Grammy-award success isn't strong. Hope this helps. Please call if you have any questions or concerns. And thanks for listening. Bye."

Arthur left one more message, this last more explanatory:

"Hello, Mrs. Slow, Bryan. Don't know if you've been receiving my messages—I left a few for each of you—and, if you did, you may find them contradictory, but there's a reason for this. You've both been looking at musical stardom and attending Harvard as an either/ or situation—if one decision is good, the other is bad. The marshmallow principle, though, doesn't dictate a right or wrong path to achieving your goals—it's a method of realizing your ambitions over the long term. Armed with the information I gave you, each of you could win an argument yea or nay about Harvard and receive the instant gratification of victory. But what's in Bryan's best long-term interests? If he has ambitions beyond playing a guitar, which could include anything from starting his own record label to opening a School of Rock, á la the Jack Black film, a Harvard business degree could give him a serious edge over his competi-tors. But so could any carefully crafted and actively pursued plan that follows the marshmallow principles to sustained success. Bryan has a copy of the plan. I'd be happy to assist with the details . . . Well, you both know where to find me so call or stop by any time."

Arthur doubted he'd get an immediate reply from any of the Slows but, just to be on the safe side, he opted to leave his office and head for home where the toughest part of his day would begin: preparing to pay a stack of bills and for his visit to the beautiful Akilah by week's end. Both prospects scared him, but it was the thought of what Akilah might do to his sorry behind that propelled him out of his seat and toward home where plush leather furniture and concrete marshmallow reminders awaited.

An hour later, safely ensconced in his heated massage recliner, a calculator in one hand and a pen and notepad in the other, Arthur was anything but relaxed as he counted the wages of his sinfully shortsighted marshmallow ways.

SlowDown! Anticipated Pay, Month 1:		$8,000
SlowDown! Actual Pay, Month 1		
Pay, for one week	$829	
Auto Allowance	$300 (payable 30th)	
Total:		$1,129
Shortfall		($6,871)

Arthur knew about the seven-thousand-dollar gap—he'd done the mental math during his chat with Betty—but believed that putting the number on paper forced him to deal with his cash-flow crisis and the far more serious financial troubles the pile of mail lying on his mahogany side table would soon reveal. Arthur got up to fortify himself with a soda and Cuban sandwich and returned to his lounger and his list. He opened his mail, uncapped his pen and wrote:

PAYMENTS DUE <u>now</u>

Rent	$2,600
Car Lease	489
Utilities	167
Cable TV/Internet/Phone	112
Cell Phone	59
Credit Card	742
Total due <u>now</u>	$4,169

Arthur's current bills outpaced his current income by $3,040. Arthur knew that his money problems didn't end there—and he didn't want to face the wrath of Akilah if she did the math for him—so he reluctantly continued his quest for financial truth.

EXTENDED DEBT

Credit Card Debt	$18,540
Revolving Credit Debt	21,540
(condo furnishings)	
Thirty-Six Month Auto Lease	
Actual: $46,944	
Less car allowance: $36,000	

Net Owed (assuming I keep my job!!)	$12,984
Total Extended Debt	$50,984
(if I never charge another thing)	

Arthur gasped and nearly spilled soda on his new silk Persian rug. Fewer than thirty days as a salary earner and his debt already exceeded more than half of his anticipated annual salary. And added up to ten thousand dollars more than his take-home pay, not including commissions.

Arthur punched another number into the computer—the $31,200 owing on his twelve-month condo lease and was hit with another hard reality: his total, committed-to expenses added up to $82,184. If he added in the cost of essentials such as food, gas and a salesman's wardrobe, Arthur deserved a new title: the One Hundred Thousand Dollar Debtor.

As sobering as this realization was, Arthur actually smiled. He now had an idea for a high-stakes wager with a guaranteed pay-off. Wait until Akilah heard about it!

6

Back to Marshmallow Basics

Arthur hit the phones every morning and the pavement every afternoon the rest of the week. He chased down hot, warm, cold—even frigid—sales leads, accumulating six potential consulting contracts by week's end. One would yield a big fat commission check—big enough to pay off his debts—and Arthur couldn't wait to share his great (and decidedly bad) financial news with Akilah. So he was disappointed by her unenthusiastic reaction when they met at Study Break early Friday evening.

"You can't pay the rent with *potential* sales, Arthur. Spending money against your *potential* salary is what got you into your mess. If you've got nothing more to tell me than that, I've got a plane to catch and a *potential* fortune to make on a game of twenty-one."

"No, wait, Akilah! That's not what I came here to tell you. It's true that I sugar-spun my marshmallow horror story—eighty grand in debt—so you wouldn't be disappointed in me. And it's not like I'm going to stop making sales calls because of a few great leads. I'm going to keep working nights, days and weekends to turn my fantasy salary into reality. And I'm going to make you a wager to prove it."

"First you tell me not to gamble my savings and now you want me to place a bet with *you?* Are you on a marshmallow high or something?"

"This is a win-win bet for both of us," Arthur insisted. "We're going to make each other a promise and, as Mr. P taught me and you've heard me say often enough, 'Successful people keep their promises.' So it will be up to us—not casino odds—to win our wager."

Akilah sipped her coffee and chewed her lip before asking, "What kind of wager and what kind of promise are we talking about?"

"I'll get to that in a minute, but let me explain how I came up with the idea so you'll understand how serious I am. If you can just be patient for a few minutes—"

"My middle name is Patient," interrupted Akilah.

"But I'd rather have it as a last name—you know, marry that billionaire ex-boss of yours. He's rich *and* handsome. I wouldn't mind nibbling some of that man's marshmallows."

"Akilah! Can you please let me explain my plan?"

"Sure, go ahead. But just for the record, I think you're pretty too. Broker than broke, but at least that's something you can work on. Ugly's harder to fix, and plastic surgery is risky, not that you could afford it anyway, but as eye candy goes—"

"Akilah, please be serious!" Despite his own impatience with Akilah's ramblings, Arthur blushed at her compliment. But in an attempt to steer the conversation back toward his original intent, he offered her a pre-wager wager: "Akilah, if you give me five minutes of uninterrupted silence, I'll listen to ten minutes of anything you want to say. That way we both get what we want. Okay?"

Arthur accepted Akilah's silence as a handshake and launched into an explanation of his plan:

"Over the last four years, you've heard me talk about the marshmallow plan and the rewards of delayed gratification. So I know you understand the concept. But I think you could use some help in actually putting those concepts into action. Saving all that money is a great start, but what are you going to do with it? Why, when and for what purpose? I could help you—I *want* to help you—turn that first great marshmallow-resisting effort into sustained, long-term success.

"Now, I also know that as thoroughly as I understand the marshmallow principle, I stopped applying it to my life. Right now, I should be enjoying the rewards of reaching the goals I set for myself when I was working for Mr. P and putting into action the things he taught me, like, 'Purpose plus passion plus action equals peace.' Instead I'm completely stressed out because I've reduced my purpose to paying my rent with a credit card before the bank lowers my charge limit.

"I was a lot happier when I was living in Mr. P's carriage house, testing out his assertion that, if you doubled a dollar a day for thirty days, you'd have more than five hundred million dollars at the end of the month. I ended up with a mountain of marshmallows in my room before I realized I could do the calculations on a computer, but putting that single concept into action inspired me to actively shape and pursue my goals.

"That was five years ago. Today is today, and here's what I think now, Akilah. You need to form an action plan to help you realize your dream of restaurant ownership, and I need one to get back on track with my goals, maybe even shape some new ones. So I propose that we get down to marshmallow basics together. We'll share our goals and our progress. And because we both know that successful people keep their promises, we'll turn our wager into a promise, which will increase the odds that we'll both succeed. We'll teach and mentor each other. What do you think?"

"You actually think you could learn something from me or are you just puffing me up so I'll agree to whatever wager you have in mind?" Akilah asked.

"I know you have a lot to teach me, Akilah. You already taught me that I can't solve my problems by hiding from them—or paying for them with credit. And I can't believe I'm the only customer you've eavesdropped on, so I'm certain you've stored away some valuable insight. Besides, your name alone proves that you'll be as good a mentor as a mentee."

"What are you talking about?"

"Your name, Akilah, means wise, intelligent and logical. Did you know that?"

"No one ever told me that before," Akilah said, "and usually just the opposite."

"That's why 'building self-esteem' might be at the top of your 'things I need to change' list," Arthur replied, "But I'm getting ahead of myself. Are you ready to accept my wager?"

"You have to make the wager first," Akilah said, "and then I'll have to think about it. It's what a wise, intelligent, logical woman would do."

Arthur laughed. "Okay, here's the deal: I promise to be out of debt and saving money within a year if you promise to keep saving your tip money to help you start a restaurant."

"All I have to do is not spend money I haven't spent in four years? That's too easy. Besides, you'd be the only one winning anything. You'd be out of debt and saving money and I'd be standing still watching the coffee urn collect dust."

"But, with my idea, you wouldn't be facing any risk."

"Or any gains," said Akilah. "No, Arthur, I don't accept your wager—and it doesn't even sound like a wager—but I'll make one of my own. I bet that I will double my savings in a year. You'll bet that you will be out of debt and be able to match my savings in the same amount of time. That will be the bottom line of the bet. A year from today, we will each have a minimum of $10,268 in the bank. If we don't reach that goal, the bet's off and we can keep our money and do whatever we want with it. On the other hand, if we go beyond that goal, the one who surpasses it the most gets to tell the other what to do with the money."

"Wait a second, Akilah, you're confusing me. First, where did you get the ten thousand dollar figure?"

"I counted the money in the urn—$5,134—and put it in the bank." When Arthur raised an eyebrow, she said, "Did you really think I was going to gamble all that money away in Vegas? I was angry, but I'm not a fool, Arthur. Anyway, it took me four years to save that money, and I'm betting I can double that savings in a year. You have to put the same amount in the bank *and* clear your debts within a year's time."

"And whoever has the most money saved at the end of the year—provided we both save more than the $10,268 minimum—gets to tell the other what to do with his or her money. Is that right?"

"Yes, but there are two more conditions," Akilah countered.

"You're a tough negotiator, Akilah, and I can't believe you thought up this wager off the top of your head just now. How long have you been thinking about this?"

"A wise woman doesn't share all of her secrets," Akilah said, laughing. "Now, do you want to hear about the other two conditions?"

"Do I have a choice?"

"Stop whining. I think you'll like the conditions, at least the first one, and you definitely need the second to have a chance of winning the bet."

"Okay, I'm listening."

"No, I'm listening," Akilah teased. "The first condition is that you have to tell me a story—a *new* story, one you've never told before—that will inspire me to reach my goal: owning a restaurant."

Arthur smiled. Akilah wasn't the only one who'd come to the meeting prepared. He'd spent hours surfing the Internet for success stories that he thought would give Akilah the boost she needed.

"First, a question: besides me, how many people have you told about your desire to own a restaurant?"

"No one. Everyone around here would just make fun of me and—"

"And have you kept this idea in your head or have you written it down?"

"In my head, Arthur. It's not like I'm going to forget. I don't need to remember that I want to own a restaurant."

"It's good to have a goal in your head. There's an old Harvard study that found that graduates who had goals but didn't write them down earned twice as much as those who didn't have goals at all. But the three percent of the graduates who had clear, written goals earned an average of *ten times* as much as the other ninety-seven percent of graduates combined."

"That makes pencil and paper a good investment," Akilah said. "You've got my attention, but I need more than studies and statistics to get motivated. Tell me a story."

"Coming right up," Arthur said. "You've heard of Ellen DeGeneres?"

"Of course. I love her. She's a very funny lady. And really successful," Akilah said. "Go on."

"She's someone who strongly believes in—and proves the power of—writing down goals, sharing them with others and, as she says, 'putting them out into the universe.' Recently she's started sharing her life list with millions of people—her viewing audience."

"She writes down goals? Really? I thought writing down goals was just something you corporate types did at those rah-rah seminars your bosses forced you to attend."

"Writing down goals—and picturing them as realized—is something successful people in all walks of life share in common. And successful in all kinds of ways. People who've posted pictures of their dream houses on their bulletin boards and written down the desired traits of their ideal mates have gone on to live in homes and marry partners almost exactly as they'd envisioned. So it's not just business or financial success that can get a boost from written goals . . . But back to Ellen—"

"Yes, please," Akilah said. "Although I will hold on to that idea of ordering a perfect mate . . ."

"Back to Ellen," Arthur continued. "Her bio boasts that she was the first—and only—woman to be invited to sit down with Johnny Carson on a first visit to *The Tonight Show*. But long before that ever happened, when she was still doing stand-up comedy in her hometown of New Orleans, she laid out the entire sequence on paper and in her head. Although few comedians—and no woman—had ever been invited to Johnny Carson's 'hot seat' before, Ellen knew it would happen even though she didn't know when."

"But she must have been just a kid then," Akilah countered. "Isn't every would-be celebrity's dream to be invited onto a talk show? Didn't she just have a fantasy that happened to come true?"

"Maybe, but her now-I-see-it-now-I-achieve-it story doesn't end there. She appeared on *The Tonight Show* more than twenty years ago, but she's continued to prove the power of writing down goals even when logic—and the popular press—suggested her goals were impossible."

"What do you mean?"

"Back in 1997, when Ellen announced that her television character and she were gay, her career took a very sharp downturn. No one was calling her the funniest person in America anymore—a title she earned after winning a Showtime contest in 1982—and some, instead, were calling her names like Ellen Degenerate. Her once successful show was canceled, another failed after a single season and a lot of people were happy when she seemed to disappear from public view."

"She did kind of go away and then, suddenly, she had a talk show and was winning Emmys and hosting the Emmys and—"

"There wasn't any 'suddenly' about it. The thing is, Ellen never lost sight of her goals. She kept writing them down and kept envisioning her success. She also kept working, by the way, writing a book that became a bestseller and returning to her marshmallow basics—stand-up comedy—but even though her marshmallow path had changed, her goals didn't. As she said, 'I'm a writer and a performer and I love making people laugh. This is what I'm meant to do. It's where I belong. I can't run away from it.'

"And ten years after the darkest part of her career, she realized two lifetime ambitions—working with animals and hosting the Oscars."

"Working with animals? Oh yeah, those American Express commercials," Akilah said, adding thoughtfully, "So, you're saying it took more than talent and ambition for Ellen to succeed. Or even luck. She created her own success by writing down her goals, imagining great outcomes even when no one else did and taking action to achieve what she wanted?"

"What I'm especially saying is *you* can do it too, Akilah. Start writing down your goals today and when you go to sleep tonight, dream about that restaurant you'll own someday. Picture it down to the napkin holders and chair covers. See a goal vividly in your mind, and you can achieve it."

Akilah started to protest, to tell Arthur that Ellen De-Generes had never faced the obstacles she, herself, faced, but she kept quiet. In the first place, maybe it wasn't true and, more important, maybe Arthur was right. Maybe she needed to stop focusing on the roadblocks and start thinking about her destination. Winners form the habit of concentrating on what they want to happen; losers concentrate on what they don't want to have happen. In pressure situations, winners call up past wins; losers recall past losses. Both are self-fulfilling.

"Good story, Arthur, and I'll tell it to myself before I go to bed tonight," Akilah said. "Now, there's just one more thing you have to do before we have a deal."

"Another story?"

"No, take this," Akilah said, removing a stained and slightly torn envelope from her apron pocket, "and open it. According to Mr. P, it's past time that you do."

"Where did you find this? When did you talk to Mr. P? How do you—"

"It's a long story and not important. Just agree to open the envelope, and we've got a deal. I've already got plans for *your* money when I prove I've got more in my savings account than you."

Stunned that Akilah had reunited him with his gift from Jonathan Patient and shocked that the two of them had been talking—*does he know I've been gobbling my marshmallows?*—Arthur accepted the envelope without further comment.

He waved a weak good-bye to Akilah, left the restaurant and, secure in the privacy of his car, started to open the envelope. But, before he had completely broken the seal, Arthur hesitated, then shoved the envelope into the glove box. Arthur would keep his promise to Akilah, but not just yet. He was too shaken by what he'd just learned to risk discovering something that might be more unsettling. The secret would remain inside the envelope for now.

7

Dinner with Jonathan Patient

Six weeks later, Arthur sat in the back of Jonathan Patient's limousine behind his old boss's new chauffeur.

"What's this all about, Miguel?" Arthur asked, absentmindedly buffing the leather with his jacket sleeve. "Where are we going and why?"

"All I'm supposed to tell you is that Esperanza is making her world-famous paella and she's promised you'll get the serving with the most *langosta* (lobster)."

"Mr. P knew I couldn't resist my favorite meal no matter what the consequences. What else did he say about this mysterious meeting?"

"Not to say anything else," Miguel responded firmly. "And since I want to keep my job, I'm going to keep my mouth shut . . . except to tell you to stop polishing the seat cushions. I cleaned them before I came to fetch you."

"No offense intended, Miguel. The car is immaculate." Arthur shrugged. "Old habits die hard, you know? And, in my case, they get resurrected from the dead."

•   •   •

Jonathan Patient stood in the doorway of his estate and Arthur loped across the driveway before Miguel unlocked the driver's door. The men hugged hard and with heartfelt emotion until Arthur, anxious to discover the reason for this reunion, broke the embrace.

"I've never known you to answer your own door," Arthur said. "Did the maid quit?"

"I've never known you to run so fast," Jonathan said. "Are you that hungry for paella?"

"No," Arthur answered truthfully. "I've just really missed you and I shouldn't have stayed away so long."

"I've missed you too, Arthur, and I'm glad you're here now. Come inside. I have a surprise for you."

Jonathan led Arthur through the foyer and front room, down the hall and through a pair of French doors into the formal dining area. The linens, the silver and china were exactly as he remembered and expected to find—Mr. P was not a fan of redecorating—but he was completely unprepared to find six familiar people seated at the table:

Akilah, Bryan and Mrs. Slow, Esther, Ed and even Amy, whom Arthur thought was on a business trip in Hong Kong, sat smiling at him. The only empty seats were Jonathan's usual place at the head of the table and one at the opposite end.

Arthur gulped, suddenly terrified. "What is this, some kind of intervention or something?"

"No, it's just a dinner party with a purpose," Jonathan said, then smiled. "Relax and take the guest of honor's chair," he said pleasantly. "The paella's ready to be served. Later, while we're enjoying your favorite chocolate cake and espresso, I'll tell everyone why we're here tonight."

Despite his near panic, Arthur couldn't help but savor the joys of Esperanza's cooking. Between courses, he excused himself to the kitchen to give her a hug. He was tempted to stay there, but before he could sample even a bite of cake, Esperanza shooed him back to the dining room.

• • •

"Welcome back, Arthur," Jonathan said smiling. "I hope you left some dessert for the rest of us."

"Esperanza made sure of it, Mr. P—Jonathan. She said she'd be serving in a minute, but I don't think I can wait that long to find out what you have to say. Can you tell me now, please?"

"Certainly, but first I have a test for you," Jonathan began. "You recall that you gave Bryan a copy of The Six-Step Marshmallow Plan to Sweet Success in Anything—and Everything!"

"Sure, that was the last time I ever heard from him," Arthur said.

"I heard a great deal from him and all of your friends here," Jonathan said. "And it turns out that all of them are familiar with the plan—you've been a very good mentor, Arthur—so it was easy for me to ask them to complete an exercise in preparation for this meeting."

"Everyone's been *preparing*, except me?" Arthur groaned. "And now I'm the one who has to take the test! You've never been anything but kind to me, Mr. P. I hope you're not going to show me a different, mean side tonight."

"Not mean, but well meant," Jonathan said. "Now, getting back to my explanation, I asked everyone here to concentrate on just two parts of the plan—defining your goals and your willingness to achieve them—and I asked them to do this for thirty days in a row without ever reading what they'd written before."

"Okay, I understand," Arthur said. "So what's the test?"

Esperanza, who'd finished serving dessert, carried an easel into the room and handed Jonathan Patient a marker. He walked to the easel and on the left side, wrote:

Play at Carnegie Hall
Go to Harvard
Own a chain of restaurants
Open a free clinic for animals
Open an accounting firm in Hawaii
Marry the person I love

"Okay, Arthur, it's your turn at the easel. Match the goals to the person to whom you believe it belongs."

"Sure. This will be easy," Arthur said, quickly adding names to the right-hand column:

Play at Carnegie Hall	Bryan
Go to Harvard	Mrs. Slow
Own a chain of restaurants	Akilah
Open a free clinic for animals	Esther
Open a surfing school	Ed
Marry the person I love	Amy

"I kind of guessed at the last one," Arthur said, "but Amy was the only name left. So how did I do? Did I get them all right?"

"Actually, Arthur, you only got two of them right," Jonathan Patient said.

"Two? That's impossible. Most of them are so obvious—"

"I know you're surprised, Arthur. So was I. But I was delighted at the success of the exercise. And I believe you will be as well. But you shouldn't hear the stories from me. The goal-setters should tell the stories themselves."

Arthur looked first at Bryan but, since he'd guessed wrong, he looked at Esther, remembering how much she loved to play the drums. It was Mrs. Slow, however, who spoke:

"Despite what you probably thought, Arthur, I didn't dismiss what you said to me in your office and I didn't ignore all the messages you left on our answering machine. In fact, there's one in particular I played over and over again, not realizing its significance until I talked to Jonathan and sat down and started writing out my goals."

"What message was that, Mrs. Slow?"

"Please, call me Rose. It was a message intended for Bryan, the one about the guitarist who spent eight hours a day practicing guitar while at Harvard. And then I came across an interview by Tiger Woods, and he talked about practicing golf for eight hours a day, not because he has to but because he loves the game." Rose Slow took a deep breath and continued:

"I learned two important lessons: the first was that passion would propel Bryan to be great in whatever career he chose so I knew it was wrong to force him to go to Harvard or do anything else. The second was that I needed to focus on my goals—not Bryan's—and when I did, I realized that I want to pursue a goal I abandoned long ago—to perform a piano recital at Carnegie Hall."

"But, Mom, you don't even play the piano—" Bryan interrupted.

"Not that you'd know of," Rose Slow said. "But there was a time before you were born when I played happily—blissfully—for eight, ten hours a day. I turned down a scholarship at the Juilliard School in New York. After that, I was certain I'd forfeited my only chance at great musical success, so I abandoned the piano entirely.

"But thanks to you, Arthur, and your mentor's urging, I realize I can and will make it to Carnegie Hall."

"That's astoundingly great news," Arthur said. "But now I'm confused. If Harvard isn't your goal, whose is it?"

"Mine," said Bryan, blushing. "That 'eight hours of practicing' message had the exact opposite effect on me. Sure I love the guitar, but when the idea of practicing all day sounded like *work*, I thought I needed to really think about whether guitar was an interesting hobby, a potential career or just a way of rebelling against my parents. When I couldn't even commit the time to complete a budget for a road trip to Hollywood, I knew I wasn't ready to declare myself a rock superstar. When it came to the 'what are you willing to do?' part, I mostly drew a blank."

"I'm impressed by your maturity, Bryan," Arthur said. "But why did you decide to accept Harvard's offer?"

"Because it *is* a great opportunity and a chance for me to really explore where my passion lies, what I want to do for eight or more hours a day that won't feel like work. Plus, even though I mocked my SAT scores, it was secretly pretty cool to find out that I was smart and maybe when I'm in a place where intelligence is accepted—and expected—I'll develop the confidence to do things I never thought I could.

"Mr. P told me a story about circus elephants that really impressed me," Bryan continued. "He said that, before and between shows, elephants stand tethered to small posts by weak ropes. And he asked me why the elephant never tried to escape. My first thought was that the elephants liked living in the circus, but that didn't make sense—elephants are born to run in the wild not be imprisoned inside a tent. Mr. P said I was right—the elephants hated the circus—but they'd come to believe they couldn't escape, so they stopped trying. They'd been tied up like that when they were babies and, when they were small, they couldn't break free no matter how hard they tugged. One day, the elephants just stopped trying although, as they grew bigger, a single pull would have set them free."

"That's a great story, one Jonathan never told me," Arthur said. "How did you apply it to your own life?"

"I won't go into the whole story, but back when I first started school, I took some tests that 'proved' I was mentally slow—not fundamentally challenged but definitely back-of-the-room material. Anyway, it didn't take me long to stop believing I was smart, so I stopped trying. I never even studied for the SATs, so I didn't know what to expect from them. And because I hadn't set myself up to fail them, I ended up doing really well. Without even realizing I was tugging at the rope, I set myself free. And now I want to explore life in the 'wilds' of Harvard and start over with a new perspective."

"You gained the courage to move away from your comfort zone," Arthur suggested.

"Exactly," Bryan said. "Going on tour with my band without any plan except to make it to Hollywood would have kept me in my comfort zone—the anything goes zone—but I need a real academic challenge, so my goal is to graduate from Harvard—with honors."

"That's terrific to hear, Bryan, it makes me feel a lot better about confusing your goals with your mom's. But the chain of restaurants—that has to be you, Akilah."

"No, not me," Akilah said. "I want to open one restaurant, the most successful one in Miami, but I never said anything about owning a chain of them. Unless I wrote that down accidentally?"

"No, you didn't, and neither did I," said Jonathan. "So who's the future restaurant mogul in our midst?"

"That would be me," Amy said. "All the traveling I do has given me some killer ideas about fine and not-so-fine dining. My father is a culinary chef, and I love to eat . . . although there's tons I don't know about day-to-day management. So, Akilah, maybe we could put our heads together and come up with the best restaurant in Miami—and the world!"

"We should definitely talk," Akilah agreed, "but let's watch Arthur continue to prove how much he doesn't know first."

"Ha, ha," retorted Arthur, "but I *know* I'm right about the next one. You want to open the free pet clinic, right, Esther?"

"Yep, I'm the one. I've known since I was thirteen that I was going to spend my life working with animals and the only thing that has changed over time is how. When I was a kid, my mother owned two beautiful poodles, Mr. Big and Nina. She met a very nice man who became my stepdad and he too fell in love with those two puppies. Mom and Dad even let the dogs sleep with them in their bed. One day Mr. Big fell and broke his leg. My mother was frantic and rushed him to the emergency room of a pet hospital. Mr. Big had to undergo surgery; a metal rod was inserted in his little leg to hold it together. For three months my mother nursed that dog back to health. She carried him everywhere, cradled in her arms as if he were a baby. It was then that I understood how much people could love their pets. I decided that my mission in life would be to help animals since they give so much joy to human beings. But you may be wondering why I would be interested in opening a free veterinary clinic and not a for-profit one. Well, my parents were very well off and they could afford to give Mr. Big and Nina the very best care they needed, even though it cost thousands of dollars. But what about people who have no money? Some can't afford to have a pet and they go through life without having the pleasure of having one. Others can afford to have a pet but they can't afford to give them the needed veterinary care. I strongly believe that the haves of society should help the have nots and owning a pet is one of the joys of life that everyone should be able to experience. I'm so excited about going to veterinary school I can hardly stand it, and thanks to you, Arthur, I've already started looking beyond that graduation to my long, long-term goals. My 'what am I willing to do?' list includes putting a portion of *every* paycheck toward a free clinic fund, and I *will* open one, no matter how long it takes."

"What if something gets in the way?" Arthur asked. "Like marriage, kids, financial troubles."

"Then it might take me longer to reach my goals, and I may have to change my route to getting there, but I can already see the clinic's waiting room filled with poodles, parakeets and Persians, so I'm absolutely confident the free clinic will become a reality."

"With your passion and vision, I'm sure you'll accomplish all of your goals."

"Yes, I will, Arthur, but I was a lot more nearsighted in college until I shared my dreams with you."

Arthur hugged Esther and consulted the list of goals written on the easel. He looked directly at Ed. "I've got to be right about the next one too. The surfing school is your idea, isn't it?"

"Yes, it is," Ed said carefully. "But I admit I'm still working on my goals. I've always dreamed about owning a surfing school, but like Bryan, I don't know if I'm willing to do whatever it takes to make one successful. It might just be an excuse to live on the beach."

Everyone laughed and Arthur looked at the last goal on the list. Who wanted to get married? He performed a mental checklist—and repeated it twice—before looking at Akilah.

"You want to get married? I didn't even know you were in love with anyone."

"Of course you didn't," Akilah said. "Until Jonathan told me the elephant story and showed me how my lack of self-confidence kept me from taking important risks, I couldn't face the possibility of rejection."

"And now?" Arthur asked.

Akilah stood, walked toward the easel and kissed Arthur on the mouth.

"Now, you're in trouble, Marshmallow Man. Because Jonathan taught me more than self-confidence. He also revealed the secret inside the envelope."

8

The One-Minute Success Quiz

The next day, Jonathan Patient's chauffeur visited all but one of the previous night's dinner guests. Armed with a stopwatch and six hundred dollars in cash, Miguel delivered this message to Akilah, Esther, Ed, Amy, Bryan and his mother, Rose:

FROM THE DESK OF JONATHAN PATIENT

Please help me give a gift to our mutual friend, Arthur, by taking the enclosed One-Minute Success Quiz.

The person who delivered this note will wait outside and collect your answers in sixty seconds.

In appreciation of your time and thoughts, you

will be given ten dollars for each question you answer.

If you have as much faith in Arthur as I do, you know that far greater rewards will follow.

Thank you very much for your help. I hope you enjoy the quiz. Arthur will share the results with you in a week.

JP

ONE-MINUTE SUCCESS QUIZ

1. If you could change the world or change yourself, which would you pick?

2. If something great happens in your life, who's the first person you call? What about if something bad happens?

3. When embarking on a road trip, is it more important to have a single destination in mind or a hundred maps in your trunk?

4. Which is the most important ride at an amusement park?

5. What do you remember most about first grade: excitement about learning new things

or embarrassment about not knowing the answers to questions the teacher asked?

6. You're in a forest facing two enemies and can
   kill only one—a grizzly bear or your fear of
   dying. Which would you kill?

7. What's more important, the law of attraction
   or the law of action?

8. Is it better to hoard or gobble your marshmallows?

9. When is the best time to accept defeat?

10. When Arthur veered off his marshmallow
    path, what was the biggest mistake he made?

By noon, Miguel had collected six quizzes, paid out
five hundred and twenty dollars in answered-question
fees and returned the results to his employer.

Two days later, Miguel visited Arthur at his condo.
Arthur, lulled by the sounds of the ocean and reeling
from the events from his former employer's dinner party,
didn't answer until the fourth knock.

"Hey, Arthur, you need a ride anywhere? To a hospital
maybe? I was getting worried when you didn't answer the
door."

"I'm fine, Miguel, and I wasn't expecting anyone, certainly not chauffeur service. Do you need a job—did Mr. P fire you or something?" Arthur teased.

"No, and I'm not really here to offer you a ride. Mr. P wanted me to deliver something to you." Miguel handed Arthur a large envelope.

"What's in it? Do you know?" Arthur recognized Jonathan Patient's personal stationery and his name handwritten on the envelope front. But he was puzzled and worried about its possible contents.

"Sort of, not exactly, um, you know how Mr. P is."

"Cryptic."

"Yeah, he told me not to explain anything to you, but I really couldn't if I tried."

"Ha! Sometimes you have to be a master sleuth or wear a decoder ring to figure him out," Arthur said. "But did he send any clue, any message?"

"Just one. He said, 'Tell Arthur I know he's up to the challenge.'"

Arthur groaned. "*Challenge* to Mr. P equals *impossible* to the rest of us. And it's not as if I don't have enough to think about." Arthur sighed. "Did he say anything else?"

Miguel grinned. "Yes. He said that you should stop moaning and groaning and just plunge in. I'll be back in a week to pick up the results."

Before Arthur could reply, Miguel turned and jogged

down the hall to catch a still-open elevator. Arthur closed the door to his condo, leaned his back against it, took a deep breath and tore open the envelope.

"OK, Mr. P, I'm plunging. But you'd better be there to pluck me out of the deep end if I start to drown."

Arthur walked to the kitchen, grabbed a soda and a box of cookies and headed for his favorite chair and pulled several sheets of paper out of the envelope Miguel had delivered. He popped open the soda can, took a bite out of a chocolate-chip cookie and read:

FROM THE DESK OF JONATHAN PATIENT

My dear Arthur,

A few days ago, I asked some of your friends to take a One-Minute Success Quiz and I gave them sixty seconds to complete the quiz and ten dollars for each question they answered. I'm enclosing their answers for your review.

Your challenge: ponder their answers and measure them against your own carefully considered responses. You have the luxury of time—seven days instead of sixty seconds—but a greater challenge.

Create a template for applying the marshmallow principle in times of change. Keep in mind that this will become the "laws of life" for your best friends, your possible life partner and, most important, for you.

I have absolute faith in your ability to find the answers you need. So in case Miguel didn't deliver my message along with this package: allow yourself one moan, one groan and one heavy sigh and then get to work!

Fondly,
Jonathan

Arthur decided he couldn't stomach both chocolate-chip cookies and the rest of the envelope's contents at the same time, so he set the box of cookies aside, took a gulp of soda and read the results of the One-Minute Success Quiz. Ten questions, fifty-two responses. What was Arthur supposed to make of this information? He had no answers and too many questions of his own.

He knew he'd get nowhere if he just let his questions rattle around in his already throbbing head, so Arthur pulled out his large dry erase board, the tool he'd used in college to keep track of his goals and teach the marshmallow principle to his pals.

He'd deal with the questions about amusement parks and grizzly bears (where did Mr P come up with this stuff?)

soon enough, but first he had to satisfy his own concerns about the purpose of his task:

With a broad-tipped marker, Arthur wrote these questions on the left side of the board:

- Why did Mr. P insist my friends complete the test in just one minute?

- Why do I get a week to complete the same quiz?

- Why did Mr. P pay my friends up to a hundred dollars to take a one-minute test and give me nothing?

- What am I supposed to learn from this exercise?

Arthur paced, marker in hand, as he considered the first question. Mr. P was a master game player, but his sense of humor masked a serious purpose. So he knew there was nothing frivolous in Mr. P's insistence that each of the questions be answered with a few moments' thought. Why, then, was Arthur given a week to consider the riddles? Did Mr. P think he was more dull witted than his friends? A tempting thought, but Arthur knew that wasn't it. Mr. P would never send him a message of failure so what was his point?

With the words, *message* and *failure* bouncing in his brain, Arthur settled on the answer to both of the first two questions at the same time.

My friends wrote answers based on messages that had been implanted in their brains since before they could think for themselves—messages that may or may not be helpful to their successes. Mr. P's giving me a chance to evaluate those messages and change the ones that stand in the way of our success.

Arthur returned to the board and, on the side opposite the questions, he wrote:

Measure the impact of the messages you tell yourself each day and change the ones that are impeding your success.

Arthur considered why Mr. P had set a dollar value on his friends' answers and not his. Maybe it was to impress upon them the importance of the quiz, maybe to propel them to answer without thinking, maybe just as a courtesy for interrupting their work days. Ultimately he decided it didn't matter. He wouldn't have accepted payment, despite his financial predicament; he would hold out for the greater profit of learning something from this exercise. What was he supposed to learn? He remained uncertain, but trusted the knowledge would help him recover from his marshmallow meltdown and figure out how to apply the principle of delayed gratification to all aspects of his life, all the time.

Wow, I think I've learned something already, Arthur

marveled. *I'm starting to believe it's possible to get past my recent mistakes and get back on top of my marshmallow game.*

Arthur added to the right side of the board:

Don't be defeated by your mistakes. Learn something and move past them.

Buoyed by his quick progress, Arthur decided he was ready to review the quiz results. He committed to studying one question at a time so he could focus his attention on each individual task rather than rushing to make sense of the entire test. He looked at the answers to the first question of the One-Minute Success Quiz:

1. **If you could change the world or change yourself, which would you pick?**

Six answers, all the same. Everyone wanted to change the world. It made sense, of course. With six seconds to think about it, Arthur would have given the same answer. But since Mr. P was doing the asking, Arthur didn't believe that the easy answer was correct. So the answer had to be "change yourself" but why?

Arthur considered: what if the opportunity was a one-time-only deal? If you could change the world just once, would that guarantee sustained success and happiness? What if you changed your mind about the changes? Yesterday Arthur loved chocolate-chip cookies. Today, he couldn't face more than one bite of them. What if he created a world full of chocolate-chip cookies one day and woke up craving chocolate ice cream the next? And what if he liked the changes he created in the world? What would stop the world from changing anew all by itself?

Arthur returned to the board and wrote:

> If your world is changing, so what? What's important is how the change is affecting you and what you choose to do about it.

Feeling pretty pleased with himself, Arthur read the answers to the next question:

2. **If something great happens in your life, who's the first person you call? What about if something bad happens?**

Arthur saw his own name given as an answer five times, in both the bad and good news categories, an equal number of entries for mothers and a couple names he didn't recognize.

The answers didn't give him much insight, so he asked himself the same questions. His answers were Mr. P and Akilah. Akilah always seemed to give him what he needed at the moment—a pat on the back or a kick in the butt—and Mr. P gave him the tools he needed to succeed in the long term.

Arthur decided what each of them gave him was support—unlike his old poker buddies, who gave him excuses and took his money—and he returned to the board to write:

> Surround yourself with supportive people. They will be your greatest assets in good times and bad.

Arthur returned to the kitchen for another soda and ordered a pizza by phone. He needed something more than carbonated water to sustain him through what he predicted would be a long night of pondering. While he waited for his thin-crust pepperoni pie to arrive, he let his mind wander to Akilah, her shocking announcement and the memory of her kiss.

Maddeningly, the kiss was just that—a memory. Akilah had insisted Arthur take time *alone* to process her life-altering proposal and made him promise not to call or contact her in any way for a week. Of course he hadn't listened, and Akilah had been prepared. Every time he called, he was greeted with a voice mail message about the rewards of delayed gratification and taunting reminders that she knew the secret in the envelope—and other secrets too! The message concluded with a stern warning: "I know you can't resist calling—I am irresistible—but you're only going to hear this message nine times. If you call a tenth time, Arthur, I'm changing my number and my home address."

Arthur had given up after the eighth try (in case he had miscounted the number of attempts) and surrendered to Akilah's directive to ponder her proposal on his own. Now he had both her proposal and Mr. P's assignment to consider over the next seven days. It couldn't be a coincidence. Mr. P must believe he'd discover the keys to his career and love life success within the riddles of the quiz. If the two most important people in his life had gone to this much trouble to help him, he would commit to helping himself.

So, after his pizza arrived, Arthur savored a slice and reviewed the next quiz question:

3. **When embarking on a road trip, is it more important to have a single destination in mind or a hundred maps in your trunk?**

Four of Arthur's pals had answered "single destination" and two had opted for the hefty supply of maps. Arthur trusted the majority answer on this one, but wondered why Mr. P had posed the question and what it had to do with success. Midway through his second slice of pizza, he had an "aha" moment and rushed to the board to add to his list:

If you want to be successful, begin with your goal in mind. You have to see a goal to achieve it.

Arthur was amused but confused by the answers to the next question in the quiz:

4. **Which is the most important ride at an amusement park?**

There were votes for the merry-go-round, the roller coaster, the Ferris wheel and something called Death Drop.

Arthur knew from long-ago conversations that Mr. P disliked amusement parks and hadn't been on any rides since his nanny had strapped him into a horse saddle on a carousel that was stopped after its third spin when a howling young Jonathan insisted.

So, what point was Mr. P trying to make? The merry-go-round that terrified Mr. P as a toddler was considered the tamest ride by many park goers. And some people would line up for hours to go on rides like the Death Drop. Maybe it wasn't the particular ride that was important but whichever one was scariest to an individual. What did it mean in terms of success?

Arthur finished his pizza and took the empty box to the Dumpster outside his building. He remembered how much he hated garbage bins as a child—he was *certain* he'd discover a rotting corpse or a hundred-pound rat inside—and how relieved he'd been when he'd finally gained the courage to open a Dumpster lid and find its contents ordinary.

Arthur returned to his living room, happy that his neatness had helped him solve the fourth riddle. On the board, he wrote:

Face your fears. Control them or they will control you.

Arthur looked at the next two questions together. He was starting to recognize at least one theme to the quiz:

5. **What do you remember most about first grade: excitement about learning new things or embarrassment about not knowing the answers to questions the teacher asked?**

6. **You're in a forest facing two enemies and can kill only one—a grizzly bear or your fear of dying. Which would you kill?**

Four out of six people remembered embarrassment and five of them said they'd kill the bear.

The common theme, Arthur realized (and the key point Mr. P must be trying to make), was that fear—of failure, of ridicule, of poverty, of rejection, of death—kept people from taking the risks they needed to get ahead.

Killing the bear would be a temporary (and maybe vital) fix, but if you could face your fear of dying, maybe you'd find another solution. You could run, play dead, climb a tree or offer the grizzly your lunch. Maybe you could do nothing and the bear would get bored and turn away. If you took control of the fear, you could command the situation, then and in the future. What if you used your one-shot chance to kill the grizzly in front of you only to find another one behind? You'd have no weapon and would be too panicked to think your way to safety.

With these thoughts in mind, Arthur returned to the board and added to his list:

Kill your worries before they kill you.

Just four more questions to go! Arthur couldn't believe his fast pace on the project. Did he really need a week to take the quiz? Arthur took a short break to catch the sports scores on the local news, and, satisfied that his alma mater was doing well in the standings, he returned to his review of the quiz.

7. What's more important, the law of attraction or the law of action?

This question earned three votes for "attraction" and two for "action" and one comment of "I can't choose."

"I'm really not getting much help from my pals," Arthur said with a groan. "Were they guessing, relying on instinct or too pressed for time to give the question any thought?"

There was a difference between trusting your intuition and making snap judgments—Mr. P had taught him that—so he had the easy answers in front of him. What was the most important one?

"The law of attraction is important," Arthur thought. "If we want good things to happen to us, we have to believe we deserve them. We can't succeed if we focus on failing. We can't meet great people if we spend all of our time with losers. For better and, too often, worse, we tend to attract what we think about most.

"But I could sit here all week thinking great thoughts about this 'laws of life' stuff and they'd go to waste unless I did something about them. My credit cards won't get paid off just because I think debt-free thoughts. So, obviously, action is critical. But is it more important?"

Two hours passed as Arthur tried to choose between attraction and action. Just like one of the quiz takers, he couldn't choose. Maybe that was the answer. It was nearly midnight when he added his next entry to the board:

Attraction and action are like dreams and goals. You need vision to imagine your destination, but you have to take action steps to achieve your aims.

Arthur reviewed the next "or" question on the quiz:

8. **Is it better to hoard or gobble your marshmallows?**

One person said hoard, two said gobble, two filled the answer space with question marks and another wrote, "Neither."

With very little consideration, Arthur decided that "neither" was the correct answer. You should never gobble your marshmallows—Arthur was painfully aware of the price he was paying for his recent excesses—but you should be able to enjoy them.

The marshmallow principle was based on the idea of holding out for what you really want and building a surplus of whatever you value most, but there are meant to be rewards. Hoarding isn't the same as saving. Hoarding all your money might be good for your heirs, but why strive for financial independence if you don't enjoy *any* of your riches? With confidence, Arthur strode to the board and wrote:

Don't gobble your marshmallows, but sample and savor the rewards of delayed gratification.

Arthur was tired and he had important clients to meet in the morning. But he knew he wouldn't sleep until he at least considered the remaining two questions. He performed a series of push-ups to stretch his muscles and send some oxygen to his weary brain before reading the ninth question:

9. When is the best time to accept defeat?

Two people had answered this question with a bold-faced, underlined, all-caps "NEVER!" The others had left the answer blank. Were they undeclared defeatists or had they simply run out of time?

Arthur agreed that "never" was a good answer, but he believed there was a better one. There was a difference between giving up on yourself and changing strategies or goals. If you auditioned for every season of *American Idol* and never made it to Hollywood, it doesn't mean you have to give up on your dream of becoming a pop star, Arthur reasoned. But maybe it would be wise to try a different path to success—join a band, play small clubs, try out for other contests—and ask a professional singing coach to evaluate your voice. If your talent doesn't match your passion, get training or find another outlet for your passion.

Arthur added this entry to the board:

Passion Plus Talent Equals Success: one without the other equals frustration.

Arthur looked at the last question on the quiz:

10. When Arthur veered off his marshmallow path, what was the biggest mistake he made?

There were only two answers to this question as well—"arrogance" and "I know, but the answer's worth a lot more than ten bucks and he has to ask me himself!" Arthur laughed. He was 99 percent certain that the latter answer was Akilah's.

There was nothing funny about the question—or the answer he would have to sort out—but Akilah could make him find the value of humor in almost any situation.

And with that thought in mind, Arthur put away his marker and the quiz for the night. He decided he'd rather drift off to sleep thinking about the joy of sharing laughter with Akilah than the misery of contemplating his mistakes.

Before he turned off the living room lamp and headed for his bedroom, Arthur reread the notes he had made on the dry erase board:

- If your world is changing, so what? What's important is how the change is affecting you and what you choose to do about it.

- Surround yourself with supportive people. They will be your greatest assets in good times and bad.

- If you want to be successful, begin with your goal in mind. You have to see a goal to achieve it.

- Face your fears. Control them or they will control you.

- Kill your worries before they kill you.

- Attraction and action are like dreams and goals. You need vision to imagine your destination, but you have to take action steps to achieve your aims.

- Don't gobble your marshmallows, but sample and savor the rewards of delayed gratification.

- Passion Plus Talent Equals Success: one without the other equals frustration.

9

The Laws
of Life

Arthur gave little conscious thought to his Laws of Life project over the next several days. He looked at his notes on the dry erase board before he left for work each morning and before he went to bed each night, but the exercise had spurred him to get serious about the bet he'd made with Akilah and, more important, to find a way to return and stay on a path to long-term success.

Among Arthur's first uh-oh realizations is that it had been several years since he'd written down any new goals. No wonder he'd been gobbling his marshmallows—he'd formed no plan beyond landing his current job. He'd crossed everything off the list of his old five-year plan but failed to create new goals.

Arthur canceled a lunch appointment the next day

and instead bought a daily planner from a bookstore close to his SlowDown! office. After grabbing a protein bar and a cup of Cuban coffee from a food cart in the lobby, Arthur spent the next forty-five minutes writing notes to himself:

I need to:

- Set new goals.

- Focus on short-term goals—finish the Laws of Life and create a money-saving budget—but keep my lifetime ambitions in mind.

- Think about my lifetime ambitions—ha, ha!

- Review them frequently. Make goal-setting a daily, not a twice-a-decade, habit.

- Find better ways to respond to change. (Accumulating crazy debt is not healthy!)

- Evaluate both my personal and professional aspirations.

- Answer Akilah's marriage proposal!!!

- Ask Akilah about the secret in the envelope.

On the sixth morning following Miguel's delivery of the one-minute quiz and accompanying assignment, Arthur decided it was time to meet with the person responsible for both. Jonathan Patient seemed only modestly surprised by his former chauffeur's unannounced visit.

"Sorry to barge in on you like this, Mr. P," Arthur began, "but I couldn't wait until tomorrow to see you. I just had to tell you about my new goals, my Laws of Life and why, if you don't mind, I'm going to keep calling you Mr. P."

"I'd ask you to take a seat, Arthur, but you seem too excited to sit in one. But, please, share your excitement with me."

"Well, first I want to thank you for sending me the quiz. It really made me think, not just about the questions and answers, but about everything. It inspired me to really think about what I want to do with my life. But you probably knew that when you sent it to me, didn't you, Mr. P?"

"You know me well, Arthur. But I know you too. You just needed some guidance and, even though you didn't ask for help, I wanted to give you a nudge in the right direction."

"It worked! I have daily, weekly, monthly, yearly and five-year goals outlined. I'm committed to reviewing them *every* day so I can change my actions or change my goals as needed. I was so busy trying to accomplish the goals I set for myself when I was working for you that I forgot to come up with new ones. So I started acting like I was at the end of my career—or a man with a few weeks to live—instead of celebrating my accomplishments *and* planning new ones."

"You gobbled your marshmallows," Jonathan Patient said.

"Exactly. I deserved to nibble some of them, and a splurge or two would have built my confidence. Instead I splurged on everything and built up my debt load."

"Everyone makes mistakes, Arthur, and too few of us admit it when we do. Fortunately you have good friends who help you acknowledge yours—and who are committed to helping you get past them."

"I'm committed to helping them too. That's why I dropped off copies of my Laws of Life to most of them before coming here this morning. It's vital to have people in your life who support you. It's one of my laws, actually. But, here, rather than telling you about the laws, you can read them yourself."

Arthur handed Mr. P an elegantly framed document and waited eagerly for him to read it:

ARTHUR'S TEN LAWS OF LIFE & HOW TO MAKE THEM WORK FOR YOU!

1. **Life rewards positive action.**
   Put your goals in writing and take steps to achieve them.

2. **Supportive people are your greatest assets.**
    Don't give anyone permission to make you feel inferior. Surround yourself with supportive people who will help keep your self-esteem in high gear.

3. **Life demands you make a choice: excuses or results. Choose results.**
    Don't try to justify your mistakes, instead take steps to correct them.

4. **Change happens. Deal with it.**
    Don't fight change. Change your reactions or actions to fit your altered circumstance, and move forward with your plans for success.

5. **You have to identify your objective before you can attain it.**
    Be specific about what you want and go for it.

6. **Don't ever give up. Success is hanging on after others let go.**
    Get up more often than you fall down. Others can stop you temporarily . . . Only you can stop your progress permanently.

7. **Worry is your enemy. Kill your worries before they kill you.**

*If a problem has a solution, find it. If a problem doesn't have
a solution, accept it. Don't waste energy worrying.*

8. **Passion + Talent = Success.**
   *Assess your desires and your abilities. Combine them and
   the money will follow.*

9. **Attraction – Action = Failure.**
   *Attraction and action are like dreams and goals. You need
   vision to imagine your destination, but you have to take action steps to achieve your aims.*

10. **Delayed Gratification ≠ Deprivation.**
    *Celebrate each day and reward yourself frequently. Sample
    and savor your marshmallows: just don't gobble them . . .
    ever!*

"This is excellent, Arthur! You've surpassed my lofti-
est expectations. I'm going to hang this in my office. And
your friends will certainly get more than their money's
worth if they apply these rules to their own lives."

"What do you mean, 'money's worth'? I didn't charge
anyone for the rules, Mr. P."

"Of course, you didn't, Arthur. But your friends believed that you would deliver something of value to them.
So they returned the money I gave them to take the quiz,

added generous contributions of their own and applied it to one of your credit card bills."

"How? Why?" Arthur stammered.

"You'll have to ask your friends about the 'how' but I know the 'why.' They appreciate your ability to motivate and inspire them, to give them clear and concise guidelines about how to make wise choices. All of your friends will owe a degree of their successes to you. They value your gift of clarity, Arthur, as I hope you do."

"You're not going to believe this, Mr. P. Well, you will believe it, because you probably had this in the back of your head all along. Anyway, I had so much fun writing the Laws of Life and felt so much better when I returned to my goal-making habits that I decided I wanted to share my enthusiasm with a larger audience. One of my long-term goals is to become a professional speaker and coach, to teach people what you've taught me. Between the wisdom you've shared and the sometimes painful lessons I've taught myself, I believe I could help a lot of people."

"You will make a wonderful speaker, Arthur. You've been a terrific coach to your friends. I'm delighted that you're beginning to recognize what I've long thought would be your true calling."

"Thank you, Mr. P, for always knowing what's best for me, even when I'm not sure myself. Which brings me to the reason why I want to keep calling you Mr. P.

I know you asked me to call you Jonathan but, although there were a lot of signs that I was losing my marshmallow mojo, calling you Mr. P wasn't one of them. It's a term of affection. Sort of like calling you Dad. So if you don't mind—"

"Of course not, Arthur." The catch in Jonathan Patient's voice belied the formality of his response. Recovering his composure, he added, "I do have a question for you, Arthur."

"Yes, Mr. P?"

"What's your answer to the final question on the quiz? What was your biggest mistake during your marshmallow meltdown?"

"I *think* I know the answer to that question, Mr. P. And I *know* you know what it is. But I'm going to ask Akilah that question when I see her tomorrow. I'm going to ask her about the secret in the envelope too, since she knows about that as well."

"Sounds as if you have some very important questions to ask Akilah. Are there any other questions . . . or maybe an answer or two you'd like to discuss with her?"

"Just one answer, Mr. P." Arthur smiled. "I have just one very important answer for Akilah."

10

The Secret Inside the Envelope

"It's time, Arthur," Akilah said as the pair sat in their now-favorite booth at the Study Break Grill.

"Time for what?" asked Arthur, dipping his fork into a piece of meringue.

"Time to deliver."

"What do you mean 'deliver'? It can't be time to del—"

"It's exactly time, Arthur," Akilah said, enjoying Arthur's anxious moment. "It was exactly one year ago today when you promised to get out of debt *and* save more money than me—or else I'd gain control of your assets."

"Oh, that," said Arthur, relieved. "I'm more than ready to win that wager."

"So how much did you save?"

"Patience, Wise One. We should take a few moments to reflect on all we've accomplished this past year since—"

"Since we discovered the secret in the envelope."

"One simple sentence that changed both of our lives for the better."

"Yeah, what was it again?"

"Ha, ha." Arthur laughed. "You've got the words embroidered on your apron."

"I do not!" protested Akilah. "I don't wear aprons anymore. But it's true that I have the words posted on the fridge—with the magnets that were a gag gift from Bryan—and I'm thinking about getting the secret tattooed on my tummy!"

Arthur pantomimed writing the words on Akilah's midriff:

Whatever you want in life, just ask for it!

"There's not enough room. Not yet anyway. But maybe in a few months."

Arthur and Akilah were married and expecting twins. By applying the "just ask" philosophy, their relationship had moved swiftly from a kiss to a wedding to pending parenthood. It was a lot of change but, so far, they'd managed it well.

Akilah had accepted a management position at Study Break, not in pursuit of higher pay—she'd earned more waiting tables—but to learn more about the business of restaurant ownership. After careful consideration, she'd decided she could learn more practical details—setting schedules, ordering supplies—as manager of a restaurant than she could by earning a university degree. To supplement what she called a paid internship at Study Break, Akilah was taking courses in accounting and entrepreneurship at a local community college.

Arthur and Akilah had discussed the ramification of an unexpected but happily accepted pregnancy and vowed that Akilah would move forward with her dream, that becoming a mother would change the course, but not the destination of her goal.

Arthur, after successfully changing his overspending ways into overachieving habits, had bolstered his sales income (and taken action on one of his long-term goals) by taking on a few coaching clients. Arthur continued to make occasional mistakes, but he learned quickly from them and, heeding the "just ask" secret in the envelope, he sought counsel and other assistance when he needed it. By asking for help, he'd been the frequent recipient of Mr. P's riddles, one of which had yielded higher pay and more free time.

"Which has greater value," Jonathan Patient had asked, "one thousand one-thousand-dollar clients or ten one-hundred-thousand-dollar clients?"

Simple math suggests they're equal—a million dollars—

but marshmallow math, Mr. P explained, adds two variables: trust and relationships.

From this advice, Arthur had stopped behaving like a "marshmallow-eating rookie" and learned, instead, to think beyond short-term quotas or expectations and toward the wisdom of building long-lasting, trusting relationships with fewer, better clients. He learned that the best way to market himself to his SlowDown! clients was to provide them with exceptional service.

This change in focus from "more clients" to "better, fewer" clients had reduced Arthur's day-to-day workload, freeing him to grow his speaking/coaching business. It had also led to another harsh lesson and a better-than-ever paycheck.

Six months ago, Jonathan had awarded a million-dollar contract to one of Arthur's competitors. When a disappointed and distraught Arthur had asked Jonathan to explain his decision, his former boss had said bluntly: "The other guy took a serious interest in my long-term needs. You, relying on our friendship, were looking for a quick, easy deal."

Always kind, Jonathan reassured Arthur, "There will be bigger, better deals, Arthur, and I'd be delighted to conduct them with you when you demonstrate that 'don't eat the marshmallow yet' is more than a catchphrase; it's a simple, but serious way to set and achieve goals, to become successful in all that you do."

From that horrible moment forward, Arthur had practiced the marshmallow theory in all of his business dealings, which was why he *knew* without viewing Akilah's bank statement that he'd won the who-can-save-the-most wager. True to his word, Mr. P had recently awarded SlowDown! a multimillion-dollar contract, and Arthur held the commission check in his hand.

"So," Arthur began casually, "I'll show you mine if you show me yours. How much did you save?"

"Despite the fact that I could no longer rely on your generous tips, Arthur, I managed to *triple* my savings," Akilah boasted. "What about you? I know you're out of debt—I see your bills now—but you've kept your savings account balance top secret."

"My savings account balance doesn't count—"

"Of course it counts! Just because we're married, Arthur, don't think I'm going to let you renege on our deal."

"My savings account balance doesn't count," Arthur repeated gently, "because it doesn't include this." Arthur removed a truly "big fat" commission check from his pocket and handed it to Akilah.

Akilah gasped at the amount. "Arthur, you never told me you were working on a deal this big. This is amazing. How could you not tell me?"

"Because telling you would have been eating my

marshmallows. It would have given me instant gratification to tell you about this potential income, but it was a gazillion times better to wait and see the look on your face when you counted the zeros on the check."

"So you've won—big time!" Akilah said. "You get to decide how I spend my savings. Have you thought about it?"

"I've done more than think about it. I've already decided," said Arthur. "I know exactly what you're going to do with your savings—and mine. You're going to open a restaurant."

"But, Arthur, the babies! We said we were going to take the restaurant off the table for a while and—"

"And now it's back on. It will take a long time to take a restaurant from conception to grand opening—the twins could be in preschool by then—but you have more than enough money to get started now."

"But what about your speaking/coaching business? You could put the money toward that. You can't abandon your own goals for mine."

"I'm not abandoning anything," Arthur assured Akilah. "I want to grow my business slowly through referrals from successful clients, so right now that business requires time and commitment, but not much money. You can't open a restaurant without substantial funds. Besides, I already have a name picked out for the restaurant—and it's one you're going to love."

"Oh, no!" groaned Akilah. "I hope it's better than those horrible paired baby names you keep bringing up—Heckyll and Jekyll, Bonnie and Clyde, Gilbert and Sullivan."

"I did consider calling the restaurant Bread and Butter or Hold the Mayo," Arthur admitted, "but the best restaurant in Miami has to have the very best name, so I picked one that will reveal the secret to its success: Just Ask!"

Joachim's Post-Parable Analysis

Just as it's easy (but ineffective) to be a yo-yo dieter, it's a lot easier to be an occasional rather than a life-long marshmallow-resister. The temptation to gobble up marshmallows never ends—prespending a check that's "in the mail," taking on easy, quick-pay assignments and neglecting more important, long-term ones, depleting your savings on an impulse luxury purchase.

As Arthur learned, marshmallow-resistance requires lifelong observance. Yes, you're going to work hard to reach your goals and you deserve to nibble the rewards of success. Don't hoard your marshmallows through denial and self-sacrifice. Celebrate your progress—including minor victories—by treating yourself to some marshmallows. But you should never gobble them!

The temptation to gobble your marshmallows will always be difficult to resist—it's normal to want everything *now*. But the temptation will grow to Garden of Eden proportions during periods of significant change—the loss of a job or the start of a new one, relocating, marriage or divorce—and this is when you will be most susceptible to veering off the marshmallow path.

So whether you're practicing delayed gratification for the first time or after a relapse into self-defeating habits, you can always return to the marshmallow theory for help.

Much of *Don't Gobble the Marshmallow . . . Ever!* focused on the plights of near and recent graduates partly because the transition from student to working adult is a universal one and partly because school (inadvertently) teaches us to be lazy when it comes to setting goals. While in school, our goals are predefined: pass a test, get good grades, earn a degree. After twelve, sixteen or more years of school, we expect others to define our goals for us and often neglect to take responsibility for our own success.

But just as Arthur and most of his friends did (we're not sure yet about Ed), we can learn how to set our own goals—from daily to multiyear—and how to employ the championship strategy of beginning with the end in mind. Remember too that there is no perfect plan or any single right course toward success. Learn how to personalize your aims and map your individual career plan.

To learn more about the marshmallow theory and to follow Arthur's step-by-step path from a marshmallow-munching chauffeur to a marshmallow-resisting college student, I encourage you to read about Arthur's beginnings in *Don't Eat the Marshmallow . . . Yet!* But you don't have to wait to get started on defining and implementing your own goals. Here is the plan followed by Arthur and his friends:

THE SIX-STEP MARSHMALLOW PLAN TO SWEET SUCCESS IN ANYTHING—AND EVERYTHING!

1. What do you need to change?
What are you doing now that is not helping you in your life? What will you commit to changing?

Maybe you need to acquire a new skill, start a savings plan or find funding to launch a new venture. Whatever you need to do, get started today!

Also consider the need for internal as well as external changes. Sometimes we can be our own worst obstacle, and our personal conceptions can hinder us in ways our real detractors never imagined. For example, my first language is Spanish, and although I have total command of the English language, I speak it with an accent. This embarrassed me, and for some years, I turned down all speaking engagements that required me to speak English.

My business partner, Dr. Guillermo Sardiñas, may he rest in peace, kept bugging me to accept them, pointing out that Henry Kissinger wasn't limited by his accent, so why should I be? Still, I was afraid of failure, of ridicule.

I was hired by a Hispanic real estate company to conduct an eight-week training program for their Spanish Realtors. Although the man who hired me said it wasn't necessary, I wanted to learn more about real estate before conducting the program and happily signed up for a free seminar hosted by Century 21, a brand name in U.S. real estate.

At the end of the Century 21 seminar, we were asked to write down our contact information and our reason for attendance. Rather than explain my purpose I wrote a note to the speaker, Jim Beggins, president of Century 21: "Dear sir, I loved your conference. If you ever need a motivational speaker to motivate your troops, I am the best motivational speaker in the United States." I turned the card in and forgot about it.

Well, a week later the phone rang, and I was told that "Mr. Beggins would like to have lunch with the best motivational speaker in the United States." I nearly blurted out, "The best motivational speaker in the United States? Who the hell is that?" until I remembered my earlier boast. Reluctantly, I accepted the invitation. During the meeting, and after I had given Mr. Beggins very good advice in regards to his public speaking skills, he asked me how I became the best motivational speaker in the world. I said to him that I had learned it at Harvard and when he asked me if I had gone to Harvard, I told him no, that I was the chauffeur of a Harvard professor. He laughed and I proceeded to tell him that I drove this professor to all of his speaking engagements and eventually memorized his speech. I told the professor that I had heard him talk so many times that I could probably deliver the speech. Well, he challenged me to deliver a speech in front of five hundred students. I had to agree or he would fire me. The professor dressed as the chauffeur and I dressed as the professor. I did great during the speech but when I finished, someone asked me a question. I had memorized the speech but I didn't know the answer to any questions. So I looked at the student asking the question and said to him, "Sir, that is the stupidest question I have ever been asked. It's so stupid, even my chauffer could answer it for me!"

Amused by the joke and impressed by the public speaking advice I offered him, Mr. Beggins made me a deal: he was about to sign a contract with another motivational speaker for a critical corporate function. But if I would speak to about ten people in his office and the demo speech was well received, he would hire me instead for the seven-hundred-person event.

When he discussed the speaking fee, I fully realized for the first time that my reluctance to conduct speeches in English was a very expensive conceit. I accepted the challenge and signed a deal to deliver a two-hour speech *in English* for a fee that was *double* what I was going to make working sixty-four hours—that's eight eight-hour Saturdays—for the Hispanic real estate company.

Right then and there, my English-speaking career was launched and soon I started including Fortune 500 companies as my regular clients. Ten years later, I also had the added pleasure of learning the name of the speaker I'd been chosen to replace: Norman Vincent Peale, who at the time, was the person I claimed to be—the best motivational speaker in the United States.

So change what needs to be changed, and never doubt your ability to do *anything*.

2. What are your strengths and weaknesses?
What do you need to improve and how can you best make these improvements?

Be honest, and be as detailed as possible. You have many more strengths than you imagine. Write them down and remind yourself of them often—even if you think an asset couldn't possibly bear weight on your success. Let's say you make terrific brownies. This may seem like an insignificant strength unless you plan to open a chain of brownie bakeries á la Mrs. Fields and her chocolate-chip cookies. You may even think of your brownie-baking skill as a disadvantage and, granted, you probably don't want to list this on your resume or application to law school. But anything you're good at is positive and may prove to be a valuable asset; you just never know what will garner admiration from a superior. Although it's more likely you'll be recognized for superlative work, you may get noticed for your culinary, as well as your corporate, skills. Maybe you'll bask in chocolate-coated compliments from your boss at the next company picnic, and while he or she is thanking you for the sugar fix, you can take the opportunity to discuss an important new project you'd like to work on.

Superlative work will carry your career for the long haul, but outside-the-boardroom talents can fast track your success. My coauthor credits an addiction to TV trivia and crossword puzzles for two career advancements:

"Once an editor told me it was my turn to work a month of night shifts. I hated working nights—my brain shuts down at sunset—and I tried to argue logically that I was more valuable to the newspaper if I worked daylight hours. When this direct appeal failed, I challenged the editor to a trivia contest: if I lost, I'd work six straight months of nights. If I won, I'd be taken off the night rotation for a year and get thirty days to work on anything I wanted. I won the bet and earned a great deal of recognition for the stories I wrote over the next month. I also turned the editor's loss into a coup. When my work garnered praise, I told everyone that the editor had fumbled an answer on purpose, that he let me win because he knew the victory would inspire me. Instead of gloating about my superior recollection of *Bewitched* episodes, I credited him with great managerial instincts. He ended up getting a promotion and—ta da!—my professional star rose along with his. He was grateful for my diplomatic lie, and I was thrilled to be given greater creative freedom.

"Another time I helped a boss win a crossword puzzle contest in exchange for a monetary raise. It started as a joke—'What's the answer to seven down worth to you?'—but when the boss replied, 'Name your price,' I did. We'd been negotiating a pay increase for a while, so it wasn't as if there was a price tag attached to my puzzle expertise, but I was able to put my strength to optimal advantage."

Give thoughtful, generous attention when writing down a list of your strengths. Be equally candid, however, when considering your weaknesses. Don't make this an ego-bashing exercise, but do be honest with yourself about shortcomings and, more important, use this opportunity to form a plan to make necessary changes.

Do you have trouble remembering people's names? This is a handicap if your job requires social skills and can be a serious detriment if you aspire to a career in sales, public relations or politics. But name recollection is a learnable skill; you needn't be burdened with this shortcoming unless you are unwilling to learn—and practice—the tricks used by successfully social people.

After you compile your list of weaknesses, ask yourself two questions: "How does this problem impact my career?" and "What can I do to resolve this problem?" If you can't (or won't) solve the problem, you might want to consider changing careers. If you are naturally reserved, for instance, you may never be comfortable in a career such as mine. Most people fear public speaking; many can overcome this anxiety enough to get by—to deliver an occasional presentation to colleagues or raise a point at a departmental meeting. But if your fear of public speaking is profound, consider an occupation in which reticence can be an asset. Consider a career in which quiet is demanded—a librarian, a scientist, a pilot or a bomb deactivator—and your former weakness will be transformed into a formidable asset.

3. **What are your major goals?**

Pick at least five and write them down. They must be measurable and have a deadline. If you can't see a goal, you can't achieve it.

A goal is a dream with an action plan attached. We can fantasize about becoming a basketball star or rocket scientist all our lives, but those dreams can become realities only if we have the talent and we take steps to achieve them. If you're not willing to do the work, then you don't have a goal. You either have a wish that will never be realized, or worse, you have a reminder of continued failure.

Ellen, for instance, aspires to be a songwriter. She's written a couple of tunes and sings them aloud when she's walking her dog or stuck in freeway traffic. But she hasn't taken any steps to get the songs copyrighted or sold and she currently has no plans to do either. If Kelly Clarkson knocks on her door, looking for her next Grammy-winning hit, Ellen's ready to negotiate a deal. But she's not pinning her hopes on such an occurrence. Songwriting is pretty far down on Ellen's list of life goals, so it's not on the list of goals she has hanging in her office or sitting on her computer desktop. Those spots are saved for goals she *knows* she will accomplish because she's willing to do whatever it takes to attain them.

Many people do, however, equate desire and attainment. How many "retirement plans" are based on betting our children's birthdates will be the six numbers picked in a SuperLotto drawing? Don't ever be afraid to dream the biggest dreams, but always keep Jonathan Patient's advice in mind: *successful people are willing to do what unsuccessful people are unwilling to do*. Whether you want to get an A on your next math test or become a millionaire before your fortieth birthday, consider what you need to do and are willing to do in order to achieve that goal.

Don't let a goal become a symbol of failure. If you know you're not taking steps to achieve a goal—and don't intend to take such steps—eliminate the goal. If you have a goal to fit into a pair of pants hanging in your closet and you haven't worn those pants in two years, get rid of the pants! Obviously at this point in your life, you are unable or unwilling to do what it takes to change your size. Accept that, eliminate the goal (you can revisit it any time) and get rid of the constant reminder that you've failed in a weight-loss plan.

Too many people set "goals" they never plan to achieve, which is self-defeating and, usually, depressing. There's a woman we'll call Florence, to protect her identity, who announced four years ago that she was growing her hair out so she could donate her tresses to Locks of Love, an organization that makes wigs for cancer patients undergoing chemotherapy treatments. Two years ago, she announced she was getting a haircut. Her hair was one inch shorter than the required length to make a donation. She got two inches trimmed off the bottom—not enough to make a difference in the appearance of her hair but just enough to take her further from her stated goal. She's repeated similar trimmings six times and, when queried, insists she's still planning to donate her hair. For five years, she's sabotaged her goal and refused to abandon it.

Sadly, but not surprisingly, Florence has repeated her goal-burning behavior in more critical areas of her life. Her stated career goal is to become a music producer. She worked full-time and attended community college so she could transfer to her dream school, one that specialized in music production. Entry requirements required that she audition and she had a choice of playing guitar or piano for the review committee. Florence studied guitar for ten years and took a fifteen-week college class in piano. Guess what instrument Florence chose to play for the judges? Piano! She didn't know how to use the piano pedals, so she skipped that requirement. She also skipped makeup and hair care and her only adornment was a bandage on her leg to cover a shaving nick. Florence made several critical mistakes and didn't gain admission into the program. She was accepted to the university, however, and has had repeated opportunities to audition again. She declined them. She's taking no steps toward her goal of becoming a music producer—she's studying journalism and working at a furniture store—but tells anyone who asks that she will someday be as rich and famous as Clive Davis.

Maybe Florence will become a legendary producer. Maybe she will become wealthy doing something else. But she needs to align her goals with the actions she's willing to take to achieve them.

What are your goals? Which ones are most important to you? What are you willing to do to achieve them?

4. What is your plan?

How are you going to achieve your goals? What strategies do you have to implement right now to stop eating your marshmallows?

If you've gotten past your wannabe status and are committed to achieving your goals, the next step is to draft a plan to achieve them.

Perhaps you'd like to own a house. Begin by writing down that goal in the positive present tense: *I am living in a newly purchased home.*

If this is a top-priority goal, hang this statement over your workspace. Better yet, include a picture of the home you imagine yourself owning.

Now ask yourself: what do I need to do in order to become a home owner?

Probably have a down payment. How much? Find out the prices of homes in your area and determine the dollar amount you'd have to come up with to secure a mortgage. Depending on where you live, the answer can be pretty daunting. In 2007, the average U.S. home cost a little more than $300,000, but prices from state to state and city to city vary greatly. In San Diego or Miami, you could pay a half million dollars or more for a modest, apartmentlike condo. In Bismarck, North Dakota, you could snatch up a five-bedroom, two-thousand-square-foot home for $150,000. (So maybe another question to ask yourself is: am I willing to move to North Dakota to buy a cheap house?)

Determine the size of the down payment needed. This number becomes part of your plan. But what else do you need? You'll need money for closing costs, moving expenses, house insurance, maybe appliances and furniture. You'll need income to cover the monthly mortgage, plus taxes and utilities. You might need to boost your credit score. Whether you want to own a home in one, five or ten years, find out *today* what you need to do to realize your dream.

5. **What are you going to do to put your plan into action?**
What will you commit to doing today, tomorrow, next week, next year to help you reach your goals?

Once you know what it takes to reach a goal, you need to break the plan down into doable steps.

To continue with the house ownership example, let's say you've determined you need a fifty-thousand-dollar down payment.

How long will it take you to accumulate fifty thousand dollars?

Break it down. If you want to own a house in five years, you would have to save an average of ten thousand dollars a year or a little more than eight hundred dollars a month or about two hundred dollars a week.

Now write down ways in which you might save or earn an additional two hundred dollars a week. Could you eat out less often, get less expensive haircuts, carpool or buy fewer pairs of shoes? Could you work overtime, start an online business, barter for services or hold a garage sale? Think of every possible way you *could* save two hundred dollars a week and then commit to committing to at least one step today.

Don't feel discouraged if your initial efforts don't add up to two hundred dollars. If you save twenty-five dollars a week by drinking coffee from the office pot rather than running to Starbucks on your break, that's twenty-five dollars you didn't have before you launched your plan. And once you commit to a goal, even in tiny ways, your motivation will spur you to find bigger, better, faster ways to achieve your aims.

6. **Persevere.**
Don't give up. If you fall down seven times, get up eight. The marshmallow principle works. Enjoy the challenge as well as the rewards of delayed gratification.

When a goal is important to you, you will achieve it, no matter how long it takes, no matter how many obstacles get in the way. You simply won't give up.

When Ellen was ten, she announced to the world (family and sixth-grade classmates anyway) that she was going to live in an A-frame mountain cabin with two dogs and write books that would make her famous. By high school, she was telling teachers to remember her name and face and to catch her appearance on *The Tonight Show*.

"My plan was to become a journalist first, which would be a practical way to earn money, increase my name recognition by writing for magazines and, as soon as I had established savings and a reputation, I'd write my first book.

"For a decade, the plan seemed on track. I earned a full-ride scholarship to a decent undergraduate school and earned my master's at a top-three journalism school. By the time I graduated, I had a new car, a down payment for a house and a writing job that afforded nice clothes and the opportunity to sock away twenty percent of my income. By my mid twenties, my savings and investments totaled nearly a hundred thousand dollars and I was debating whether to quit my job or take an extended leave of absence so I could chase my dream without the pressure of newspaper deadlines.

"But there was greater pressure at home—a psychotic husband—and by the time I escaped the marriage I was broke and broken. Eventually I landed a great writing job in a new city, started thinking about writing a book again and—bam—the dream was shattered anew when my ex followed me, stalked me and hired a hit man to kill me.

"Another escape, a life in hiding, some misplaced trust and in the summer of 2001, I had two kids, two dogs, a car and less than five dollars to my name. This may seem like the worst time in the world to revisit my goal of becoming a novelist, but it was the motivation I needed to turn trauma into triumph.

"I made some phone calls, collected on some debts and, ten days later, we were living in a three-bedroom condo in an upscale neighborhood. I had no idea how I was going to afford the rent; I just knew I needed a symbol of improved status. After that I started setting goals, beginning with the very modest goal of earning five hundred dollars a month as a freelance writer. I continued to set short-term goals—double my income every month for three months—until I felt confident enough to extend my goals to semiannual and yearly aims. I squirreled away every penny possible and added it to the untouchable novel-writing savings account.

"The important part of this story is not the drama in my life. It's that once I focused on achieving my novel-writing goal, it didn't matter how little I started with or what obstacles I faced. When I refused to give up on my dream, accomplishing it just became a matter of attending to the details. The details have changed. The idea of living alone in an A-frame mountain house now seems creepy (thanks to Stephen King's *The Shining* and *Secret Window*) but my dream has remained a constant, a must. Honestly, if my ex found me again and showed up on my doorstep when I was in the middle of a great writing moment, I'd dial nine-one-one and keep on typing. I'm that focused and that determined. Nothing and no will stop me."

The Master Plan

When you master and practice The Six-Step Marshmallow Plan to Sweet Success in Anything—and Everything! you will discover the joys of holding out for what you really want in life and will begin attaining goals with greater speed and ease than you ever imagined.

But like Arthur and his friends, you may find yourself a bit lost when your circumstances change and your life doesn't seem to fit into your plans. How do you get back on track, tweak or rearrange goals to accommodate change and *always* move forward even when the outside world seems to be pushing you backward, sideways or upside down? Using Arthur's Ten Laws of Life and my career knowledge, I've formed a more advanced plan, which includes clear, easy-to-follow steps that will help you sustain professional and personal success in times of unwanted, unanticipated and eagerly awaited change:

THE TEN-STEP MASTER MARSHMALLOW PLAN FOR SUSTAINED SUCCESS IN TIMES OF CHANGE

1. Clearly identify the change(s) affecting you.

This may seem simple—change happens when you earn a raise, lose a job, get married, have a baby. But none of us reacts to any given change in the same way. Some people won't leave the house to buy baby diapers if they've got a pimple and can't find their antiblemish cream and others confidently attend job interviews in threadbare clothes. Some people give up friends and hobbies (and self-care) when they marry and others keep full social calendars and stay fit whether single or coupled.

So first identify the obvious change, but don't stop there. Be specific about how the change has changed you. Arthur changed pretty dramatically when he landed his dream job, and he couldn't mend his ways until he itemized the ways in which he was gobbling his marshmallows.

How has change changed you and how can you curb habits or attitudes that are undermining your goals?

Consider a minor, negative change such as a bad haircut. Do you laugh it off, spend hundreds of dollars trying to undo the damage or hide under hats for the next six weeks? Do you accept the change, take positive corrective action or convince yourself that both the situation and you are hopeless and helpless?

Life rewards positive action. Maybe you need to change your hairstyle. Maybe you just need to change your attitude. But if change, small or large, good or bad, is preventing you from reaching your goals, determine *in very specific terms* what the change is and how it is affecting you. Only then can you take steps to align your action with your purpose.

2. Just ask!

The powerful success secret of asking for what you want is never more vital than during times of change.

When you experience change, internally, externally or both, you may need help reevaluating and moving forward with your goals.

Embrace change as the perfect time to closely examine what you want and ask for it. There's no downside to asking for *anything*. The worst that can happen is that your request will be denied, which means you'll be in exactly the same position as before you asked. If you ask someone for a hundred dollars and the person says no, you're not any poorer than before you asked. If the person gave you five dollars instead of a hundred, you'd be ahead. And maybe the person will be feeling generous and will give you two hundred!

So ask for what you want—an hour with a mentor, free accounting advice, study help, financial backing or a hug. Whatever you need to move forward with your goals, just ask. Sure, you risk someone saying no to your request. But if you don't ask, you've said no to yourself.

Increase your odds of getting what you want by positioning your request in a positive, direct and specific manner. Most of us give money more readily to a Girl Scout selling cookies than we do to a homeless person asking for spare change. Why? We don't need a four-dollar box of Thin Mints, and we know a dollar could buy someone a fast-food burger. We react more favorably to a perky, polite salesperson than we do to a desperate or demanding street person because we *want* to identify with the former and fear association with the latter.

So pose your requests with cheerful confidence, and you'll be amazed at how often you get exactly what you want.

3. Surround yourself with supportive people.

When confronted with change, particularly the unwanted variety, we tend to retreat to the familiar. We call our mother, a high school friend or an ex-lover. This is terrific if our family and friends support us when we're down, encourage us to pick ourselves up and pursue our dreams and promise to be in our corner no matter what.

Sometimes, though, our inner circle includes people who say "I told you so," "That was a crazy idea anyway," or "What did you expect? You're just not cut out for that kind of success."

If the people in your life do not support your ambitions, find other people! Seriously, make new friends and never allow anyone to disrespect you. If you look for people who will boost your confidence, you will find them. If you look for people who will bring you down, you'll find them. You get to choose, so, if you are unhappy with your current confidantes, distance yourself from them and align, instead, with positive people who will push you to achieve your goals.

4. Don't dwell on mistakes.

Admit errors, assume responsibility for them and learn from your mistakes so you don't repeat the same ones over and over. But don't beat yourself up over mistakes—minor or major. We can't change the past, but we are likely to repeat it if it's what we think about all the time.

If the change in your life has been negative, it's easy to become mired in "where did I go wrong?" thinking. Let's say you were fired from a job and, let's say, you deserved to be given the axe—you screwed up. You can learn from the mistake—vow never to send erotic e-mail via your company's Internet service provider, for instance—but don't label yourself a screwup or approach your next job interview with the naughty-note fiasco uppermost in your mind.

We all make mistakes. Some of the most successful people make the biggest mistakes of all. They succeed—and you will too—by focusing on the opportunities in front of them rather than the mishaps behind.

5. Take charge of change.

You don't have to wait for change to happen; you can go out and create your own. This way you can control rather than be victimized by change. And you don't have to wait for something terrible to happen before committing to change. You can make changes when you are, literally, on top of your game. Golf legend Tiger Woods, for instance, has changed his swing twice to improve his game. He took a lot of criticism for tweaking his style, and when he changed his swing for the second time in 2002, he went more than two years without winning a major tournament. But in 2005, he won his fourth Masters and by 2007, he had won twelve major tournaments—more than any golfer in history except Jack Nicklaus.

Tiger Woods said he changed his swing because "You can always become better."

Take the risk of creating change. You don't have to wait for something to break before fixing it and you never have to settle for the status quo. Just like Tiger, you can become better.

So get tweaking!

6. Own, don't lease your goals.

Many of us have talent, ambition and terrific ideas but, too often, we take a backseat when it comes to achieving our goals.

We've all heard the sad tales of actors who lost fortunes because they paid scant attention to the business side of their profession and put too much trust in unscrupulous managers. But many more everyday people never achieve success in the first place; they relinquish control of their goals to others. Brilliant high school students want to get into Ivy League universities but let their parents or friends tell them how to answer the essay questions. Savvy investors want to become real estate tycoons but pay no attention to the properties bought and sold with their money. Top-of-their-class associate lawyers want to become partners and work hard at their assignments but don't take charge of landing new clients or creating a go-to niche for themselves.

And guess what? The brightest students, the smartest investors and the greatest legal minds lose out to dimmer, dumber and lesser folks who own their goals and take charge of achieving them.

Ellen, for instance, is frequently approached by people who have an *idea* for a book they believe will help them promote their businesses or make them wealthy outright. Those who participate in the writing and publishing process always succeed; those who hire Ellen to write and sell their books and are not involved at all are usually disappointed.

"If the named author has no passion for the project, how can I compensate for that?" asks Ellen. "I can't own someone else's goals. If a person doesn't take ownership of his goals—whether it's writing a book, opening a business or earning a raise—he's forfeiting rights to someone who can't possibly match his commitment. No one who rents a house cares as much about it as its owners. Renters have a security deposit at stake; owners often have their life savings at risk. If you want to succeed, find the people who can help, but make certain you retain the majority interest."

Surround yourself with supportive people, find experts to do the jobs you can't, hire assistants to complete tasks that chew up time better spent elsewhere—get all the help you need and deserve! It pays to delegate, certainly, but it pays incredible dividends to stay in charge of your goals.

7. Go after what you really want, not what's easiest or convenient.

Our time, resources and attention are limited, so don't waste yours on items or people of no consequence.

The marshmallow principle demonstrates the power of delayed gratification. Back in the days when Arthur was Mr. P's chauffeur, his employer asked him if he'd rather have a million dollars now or a dollar doubled every day for thirty days. Arthur chose the fast million, but Mr. P gave him a quick lesson in the power of patience: a dollar a day doubled every day for thirty days equals over $500 million.

When life hands you a disappointment, it's tempting to

reach out for whatever's most immediately comforting—a pint of ice cream or a bottle of booze. When life treats you well, it's equally alluring to immediately reward yourself. We choose tax preparation companies that promise instant refunds, so we can buy a new plasma TV today and get it installed tomorrow. But if we'd waited ten days for the IRS to deposit money into our bank account or six weeks to mail us a check, maybe we would have decided to spend our money on something that would give us greater long-term satisfaction or was in closer alignment with our goals. At the very least, we could have shopped for discount or liquidation sales and read customer reviews, getting more value for our money and, perhaps, putting some of the savings in the bank.

If eating a container of Ben & Jerry's or owning the latest electronic gizmo is what's most important to you, then eat, buy and enjoy. But if you'd rather save your calories and your cash for something better, think before you splurge. And if you do make an impulsive decision, accept and learn from it. Most of us overeat and overspend sometimes; all of us occasionally get sidetracked from achieving our goals. Successful people don't let their pasts control their futures. Even if you've spent your entire life gobbling marshmallows, you can choose now to hold out for life's greater rewards.

8. **Follow *your* passion and fulfill *your* purpose to find peace.**

My passion is public speaking. I thrive on the challenge of engaging an audience and reap satisfaction when my speeches elicit laughter and applause or a standing ovation. My purpose is to share with the world the secrets of success, to motivate as many people as possible to follow and achieve their dreams. When you follow both your passion and your purpose, you will enjoy a calm confidence, a sustained and lasting conviction that everything will be okay.

Passion will push you to succeed; purpose will make all of your efforts worthwhile.

First, identify your passion. What ignites your imagination, wakes you before your alarm sounds, engages you so intensely that you lose track of time? If money weren't an object, how would you spend most of your days and nights? If you're lucky, like me, your passion has an obvious career track. But if you incorporate your passion into your career choice, you will be successful. And when you add purpose to the mix, you will be very successful.

Let's say you are passionate about golf. Unless you regularly play subseventy rounds of golf, you are probably not going to get rich as a professional golfer. Quite the opposite, golf may impoverish you. Golf is an expensive hobby, even more so if you frequently ditch work or school to spend time on the course. But if golf is your passion, get creative about making it profitable. Golfers need equipment, of course, but you don't have to manufacture or sell clubs to base your career around the sport. Are you a caterer? Golfers need to eat. Are you handy with a camcorder? Golfers love to study their swings. Match your talent with golfers' needs, and you'll have a winning combination—a new career and a profitable hobby.

Add purpose to the mix, and you will find a way to be successful no matter what. If I suddenly lost my ability to speak, for instance, I would still find a way to motivate people. I would write more or maybe I would learn sign language, but nothing would keep me from my love of helping people succeed.

In many ways, it doesn't matter what your talent is. If you have passion and purpose, you will succeed. Ellen's younger daughter, Allison, is passionate about animals and her purpose is to ensure that every dog and cat enjoys a long and happy life. She has no interest in veterinary medicine and realizes that pet rescuer is not a pay-the-bills career choice. She is entrepreneurial, however, and believes her mission will propel her to great success.

"Maybe I'll design trendy dog sweaters or maybe I'll sell cars. It doesn't matter what I do if I stay true to my passion and purpose. Think about it. If you're a dog lover and need a new minivan, who would you rather buy it from—a regular dealer or the one who pledges ten percent of profits to animal shelters? More than eighty-three million U.S. households include a cat or dog. That's an incredible client pool, no matter what profession I choose to swim in."

If you're doing something you love, the money will follow. The key is that you choose something *you* love. One of Allison's friends, Sondra, is studying to become an accountant because that's the career Sondra's mother has chosen for her. Her mom has picked out every one of her courses and chosen the business school Sondra will attend to earn a master's degree and prepare for the Certified Public Accountant exam. The problem with this goal is that it doesn't match Sondra's interests or aptitude (she had to take and retake remedial math during her first year of college). Sondra is seriously considering dropping out of school, not because she isn't bright or determined, but because she has less than zero interest in the career choice that's been made for her. Sondra's mom believes accountancy is a stable, lucrative profession, and it's true that many CPAs do well. But successful accountants love their jobs.

If you follow your passion, even if it seems silly or insignificant to others, you will do whatever it takes to become successful.

9. Turn your fears into power.

All intelligent people are afraid of something, and during times of change, our fears are likely to increase, perhaps even paralyze us. Don't let this happen to you.

First, accept that it is normal and natural to be concerned about your physical, emotional and financial well-being. Go forward anyway. Act with courage, and the fears that hindered you will propel you instead. When you confront your fears and move toward what you are afraid of, your fears diminish and your self-esteem and self-confidence increase.

How do so many smart people end up with such poor self-esteem? Here's an illustration. I give a Smart Test to my students at the University of Miami to help them understand how they, like Akilah and Bryan, may be letting poor self-esteem get in the way of realizing their dreams.

Here's the test, as given to my students, followed by my explanation of the results and its effects:

The Smart Test

I impose three conditions to taking the test, spoken in these exact words:

1. *There is to be no talking. You are to write your answer and wait for my instructions in silence.*
2. *You must work individually and not look at the person next to you, because that person might be dumber than you are.*
3. *You must work quickly. This is a speed test. If a person has the correct answer in ten seconds and another person has it in twenty seconds, the faster person is smarter.*

This is what I tell them next (feel free to take the test too):

You are at the front desk of a hotel and behind the clerk you see one hundred little boxes with a key in each box. This means that this hotel has a hundred rooms. The boxes are not numbered. The hotel clerk asks you to number them from one to one hundred. My question to you is: how many nines did you draw from one to one hundred? Get started—nine, nineteen, twenty-nine, thirty-nine . . . Keep counting and see how long it takes you. When you finish, write down your answer.

What answer did you get? The most popular answer to this question is that there are ten nines from one to one hundred. The second most popular answer is eleven. The correct answer is twenty.

Only one person in a hundred gets this correct. Why? Because I do everything possible to make my students get the answer wrong. I literally program people to fail. First, I tell people to work individually and not look at another person's answers because he or she could be dumber than yourself.

I have called you dumb and you will want to prove me wrong, so there is pressure to get the answer right. I then say nine, nineteen, twenty-nine, thirty-nine to get you going all the way to ninety-nine and when you count the two nines in ninety-nine, you will have eleven and you will stop thinking. And, finally, when I tell you that I will be counting the seconds that it takes you to figure out the answer, I place a lot of pressure on you.

Just as I programmed the students to fail this test, we all get programmed by the constant repetition of lies or half truths. "You will never be able to do that." "You're not smart enough." "Quit dreaming. Someone like you could never do that!" We are given these messages our entire lives. So we start believing them and we let these beliefs keep us from trying to reach our goals. We become afraid of failing. But we can replace these messages with positive ones and reprogram our minds.

If you've been receiving "dumb" messages from others (or yourself), you can improve your self-confidence by changing the programs inside your head. You do this by thinking yourself into new behaviors or behaving yourself into new thinking. Either you repeat positive phrases until you believe them and start acting as if it were the truth or you start behaving the way you want to be, even though you are faking the behavior, until you program that new behavior. (You can take more Smart Tests in my book *How to Survive Among Piranhas*.)

Now for the most important part of this lesson: how can you overcome your fears and turn these hindrances into assets? In other words, how do you change your programming in order not to be afraid?

To begin, list your fears and analyze them in terms of impact. Remember that those fears are the result of faulty programming. Start with your greatest fear and ask yourself these questions:

- How does this fear hold me back in life?

- How does this fear help me, or how has it helped me in the past?

- How did this fear originate? When did the initial programming take place?

- What would be my payoff for eliminating this fear?

Some years ago, I asked myself these same questions and concluded that my greatest fear was poverty. Even when I had sufficient money for all my needs, I continued to be afraid of being broke, destitute.

How did this fear hold me back? It made me anxious about taking risks with money. I played it safe in terms of employment and chose security over opportunity.

How did this fear help me? I tended to work much harder and longer than most people. I was more ambitious and determined. I studied money-making and investment opportunities. My fear of poverty was driving me toward financial independence and helped me achieve that goal when I took control of the fear instead of letting the fear control me.

Finally I asked myself the final question: what would be my payoff for overcoming this fear? My answer was that I would be willing to take more risks, pursue my financial goals more aggressively and could start my own business. By objectively analyzing my biggest fear, I began the process of eliminating it. So can you!

Resolve to face one key fear in your life, to deal with it and be done with it. Imagine how you would act if you didn't have this fear, and then act as if the fear didn't exist. Eliminate your biggest fear and the others will fall naturally away.

If a problem has a solution, find it. If a problem

doesn't have a solution, accept it. Don't waste energy worrying.

Worry is your enemy. Kill your worries before they kill you.

10. Aim, focus, action!

The first nine steps will help you take aim and decide what goals demand the greatest focus, but every plan must include the all-important A-word: ACTION.

While it is very important to have a clear idea of what you want to achieve—the clearer the better—it is only by taking action that the path to success is illuminated.

Once you have written down and prioritized your goals, commit to taking daily action toward achieving them. That's right: do something every day. Not every action has to be a grand gesture. The little things you do add up. You can start by writing down your top goals in a journal each morning. It's a simple, five-minute ritual that puts your goals in the forefront of your thoughts.

After the publication of this book's predecessor, I wrote in my daily planner: "I will sell one million copies of *Don't Eat the Marshmallow . . . Yet!*" Unknown to me, Ellen was making the same prediction in her journal. And guess what? The book, at this writing, has sold more than a million copies in Korea alone, making it to the number one spot on the bestsellers list, and it has been published in fifteen languages.

Visit your goals and act on them daily. If you spend ten minutes or ten hours focusing on your goals, you will move toward them. Don't wait for next year, next month or even tomorrow. Do something today. Read an article, make a phone call or chat with someone online about your most important goal. Visit my website, www.marshmallow book.com, to get more information on how to turn your dreams into realities. If you want to get ahead, you've got to start moving! A baby step is better than no step. And babies actually move pretty darn fast! Affirmation without discipline is the quickest way to be caught in the tentacles of delusion. Only consistent action will produce the results you want. Identify your aims, focus on the ones most important to you and act on them *now*.

Marshmallow Rewards

The marshmallow principle works. When you know what you want, focus your energies on achieving your goals and put your plan into action, you will succeed. Keep your plan positive. Focus on what you do, not on what you don't want. If you take a final exam thinking, "I don't want to fail this test," your concentration on the word *fail* sets you up for negative consequence. Change your attitude to "I'm going to do my personal best" and you change your mindset from flunking to acing the test. Switch from thinking, "I hope I don't get fired" to "I know I am getting the promotion I deserve." And when you earn that terrific score or raise, celebrate. Take some time away from your studies or work to savor your success. Reward yourself frequently and modestly. Go to one, not twenty postfinals parties. Don't spend your entire raise, but don't deposit the entire check into a retirement account.

Nibble your marshmallow rewards. They're yours to enjoy. As long as you don't overindulge, your marshmallows will continue to multiply. The marshmallow principle is based on delayed gratification, not prolonged deprivation. You can attain and sustain anything you want—financial independence, creative freedom, loving relationships—if you nibble but never gobble your marshmallows.

Authors' Note

The marshmallow principle, based on a landmark Stanford University study, is real and, similarly, the experiences of Arthur and his friends and the stories they hear are based on real-life occurrences. Here are two, in particular, whose genesis Joachim wishes to share:

The Elephant Story

Joachim told this story to Eileen Coparropa, the dominant athlete from Panama for more than a decade, on the eve of her victory in the 2002 Central American and Caribbean games.

Joachim, hired as a psychological coach by Eileen's father when the swimmer was fourteen, found Eileen in tears as she prepared for the one-hundred-meter freestyle competition. Despite Joachim's assurances, favorable press attention and countrywide support, Eileen was convinced she could never win the competition, which included the best female swimmers from more than forty countries. When she told Joachim she couldn't possibly win—she was dominant in the fifty meter, not the hundred-meter race—Joachim told her the story about the elephant that stayed tied to a post because he had given up hope of freedom.

That evening, Eileen won the gold medal and set a Central American and Caribbean speed record, which as of this writing stands. When Joachim asked her what she did to swim so fast, this was her reply:

"As soon as I hit the water, I kept thinking, I have to win, I have to win. When there were ten meters left, I saw the elephant. I saw the elephant pull the rope and run toward its freedom. And I did the same!"

The Secret in the Envelope

The life-changing secret was auctioned off for fifteen hundred dollars at a fund-raiser to assist victims of Hurricane Andrew. It was donated by Ted Nicholas, author of *How to Form Your Own Corporation Without a Lawyer for Under $75* and other books, after someone at the auction asked him the secret of his success, which includes selling more than a billion dollars' worth of products. A few years later, Joachim met the high bidder and learned for himself the secret inside the envelope: "Whatever you want in life, just *ask* for it!" The winner, by the way, said he recovered his fifteen hundred dollars and made a five-hundred-dollar profit reselling the secret for one hundred dollars to twenty others at the auction and went on to become more successful than ever.

Original Marshmallow Stories

The stories about basketball legend Larry Bird and All-Star baseball player Jorge Posada (Joachim's cousin), briefly mentioned by Akilah, are detailed in *Don't Eat the Marshmallow . . . Yet!* The first Arthur parable shares other success-driven anecdotes and is the primer, step-by-step guide to applying the marshmallow principle and enjoying its sweet rewards.

Don't Forget!

Visit www.marshmallowbook.com, where you can . . .

- Download your own Six-Step Marshmallow Plan

- Learn how to calculate your personal expenses

- Download a copy of the One-Minute Success Quiz

- Find a list of Joachim's Forty Laws of Life and his Action Steps

- Download the Ten-Step Master Marshmallow Plan

- And more!